The Menaechmi

CHANDLER EDITIONS IN DRAMA
Robert W. Corrigan, *Editor*

Classical

Antigone SOPHOCLES
Oedipus the King SOPHOCLES
Hippolytus EURIPIDES
Lysistrata ARISTOPHANES
The Menaechmi PLAUTUS

Continental

Horatius PIERRE CORNEILLE
Scapin MOLIÈRE
Tartuffe MOLIÈRE
Phaedra JEAN RACINE
Danton's Death GEORG BUECHNER
Woyzeck & Leonce and Lena GEORG BUECHNER
Camille and Perdican ALFRED DE MUSSET
Maria Magdalena FRIEDRICH HEBBEL
A Month in the Country IVAN TURGENEV
Hedda Gabler HENRIK IBSEN
Rosmersholm HENRIK IBSEN
Miss Julie AUGUST STRINDBERG
Crime on Goat Island UGO BETTI

English

Edward II CHRISTOPHER MARLOWE
Volpone BEN JONSON
The Revenger's Tragedy CYRIL TOURNEUR
The White Devil JOHN WEBSTER
The Country Wife WILLIAM WYCHERLEY
The School for Scandal RICHARD BRINSLEY SHERIDAN
All for Love JOHN DRYDEN
The Man of Mode GEORGE ETHEREGE
The Importance of Being Earnest OSCAR WILDE

Plautus

THE MENAECHMI

TRANSLATED AND WITH AN INTRODUCTION BY

Palmer Bovie

SAN FRANCISCO

CHANDLER PUBLISHING COMPANY

CONTENTS

INTRODUCTION

Titus Maccius Plautus was born at Sarsina in Umbria in 254 B.C., and died in 184 B.C. The tradition is that after early employment in the theatre, perhaps as a stage carpenter, Plautus saved up enough money to start a business venture, which soon failed. He returned to Rome and was employed by a baker, perhaps to grind flour in a mill. During this period he turned to writing plays and, meeting with success, embarked upon his career as a professional playwright. His productive period spanned the years 214 to 184 B.C.

While his plays were based on Greek models and were translations, Plautus did not simply translate his materials but rearranged and combined them, adding many distinctively Roman touches. As the product of the first Roman artist to devote his work entirely to playwriting, Plautus's comedies were warmly received and reproduced constantly. So many plays were attributed to him, the number reaching as many as one hundred and thirty, that by the time of Varro in the late Republican period it was found necessary to establish a canonical list. Varro did so, listing the twenty-one plays we have today as genuinely from the hand of Plautus. From Horace's severe opinion of Plautus's style and literary aims, it can also be judged that Plautus rated significant consideration among playwrights at the time of the "Golden Age" of Latin literature.

The other writer of Roman comedy always thought of with Plautus is Terence, his immediate successor, as it were, to the mantle of Roman Comedy. The thirty-six years of Terence's life (195-159 B.C.) saw the composition of the six comedies we still possess, which are often contrasted with the plays of Plautus. Terence himself chides Plautus for *neglegentia* and for arbitrariness in adapting his models. In so doing, he affirms the importance of his predecessor.

The two writers differ in style and mode, Plautus being the noisier and less restrained, Terence the quieter, more deliberate artist; Plautus overflowing the boundaries of his models, Terence finding these limits his best guide to composition. But both men pioneered in a rich and lucrative vein, crossing over from Greek art to Roman experiment and discovering great resources within their own new language for cultivating the sense of humor. Both handed on to later writers and readers a new expression, realized in Latin verse, of man's persistent concern for the bright side of dramatized experience.

The Menaechmi ranks among the best work of a self-confident artist with a sharp eye for the stage and a practiced hand in writing for the theatre. The profuse Latin verses race forward beguiling and exciting the ear; the giddy confusions of the plot mount to the head, until by the final scene we are as momentarily dazed as the twin brothers confronting themselves. The lines of the play, the capricious conflicts and uncanny frustrating of communication, have set swirling the age-old problem of identity. A shrewd and practical slave presides capably over the situation caused by the steady accumulation of so many errors within one brief action, and deliberately rehearses the clues like a literary sleuth. As we watch the crafty Messenio fit the pieces together and watch the twins find out who they are, we sense the timeless truth of the theatre. Illusion dissolves into reality; distance between the characters changes into proximity; a slave is not only free, but on the verge of becoming rich; two brothers are united again.

No situation could be more simply farcical to begin with. Each brother sets about managing his own situation competently, gaily, adventurously, playing his satisfactory and amusing role, But gradually, as each character in turn comes forward recognizing Menaechmus II, only to be unrecognized by him—including father-in-law and doctor summoned, if not for this purpose certainly for this effect—the confusion of recognition and nonrecognition becomes a chaos of conflicts ordered by the deft synchronization of exits and entrances. The stubbornness of Menaechmus II in not recognizing his "witnesses" upsets everyone but himself, for he is resourceful enough to pretend not to be, that is, not to recognize, himself. Since Menaechmus I has meanwhile stumbled back into this disturbed and distracted situation he can only add to the trouble by systematically recognizing everyone in sight. But by doing so he meets disaster under the auspices of recognition, where Menaechmus II had triumphed by means of non-recognition. And he aptly describes himself as "the most left-out character:" *nunc ego sum exclusissumus,* at the end of Act Four. The outsider has been taken into the situation, the insider excluded from it. By the time Menaechmus II is forced to pretend madness as a means of controlling his situation, and Menaechmus I is actually attacked and almost carried off to confinement, the errors in identity have risen to their logical climax. The escape of Menaechmus I, thanks to Messenio's timely intervention, the reappearance of Menaechmus II soon thereafter, and the final triangular confrontation, set the stage for a positively Euclidean success of mind over matter.

There is, then, much heart and thought underlying Plautus's mischief. Identity is interesting and elusive, more engrossing perhaps, if less subtle, when it is doubled. Shakespeare increased the number of problems and gained even more violence, melodrama, and threatened punishment; he took measures to offset the added force by contributing romantic and lyric elements not found in Plautus. But the main idea of the confused identities (which Shakespeare derived from the *Amphitruo* as well as from *The Menaechmi*), although more elaborately worked out and more comic in its errors, still provides the main substance of Shakespeare's comedy. When Shakespeare added love interest and pathos and increased the violence, he found occasion not only to compose beautiful lines keyed in the dialectic of love poetry, but also to change over to outrageous puns and obscenities (even adapting Latin to this purpose), to transform the characters of the twins into those of gentlemen with English sensibilities, to turn Plautus's doctor, an authority on madness, into his own Pinch, a schoolmaster, and often to alter and complicate the original play of Plautus beyond easy recognition. But the fundamental interest still derives from the dramatic pursuit of identity, from the discovery of the actual persons responsible for the action, from the reversal of their sad state of affairs to a happy one.

Plautus's technique may, of course, best be studied in the annotated editions of the Latin play and in the extensive critiques of his art written by scholars of the subject. These sources generally award Plautus great credit for inventiveness and facility in language and diction, for mobilizing the powers of Latin for ardent, vigorous expression. It is a daring and exciting sphere, the world of Plautus's language, perhaps reflecting to some extent the state of mind of the new Romans, successful as a nation now having met the challenge of Hannibal and neutralized military rivals in the East. A new sense of dominance in the Mediterranean, unhoped-for signs of commercial prosperity dawned on the Romans after the early centuries of privation and struggle. Plautus seems gifted with an analogous sense of power in his art.

He strikes here and there freely and energetically, Romanizing the Greek externals of his models, adapting, changing, consolidating, claiming the new territory of comedy for his own. As a versifier he gains expert control over the medium while it is still at an early phase of its development, close to the accentual cadence of Latin but capable of being shaped and moulded by meter. He builds his verse lines solidly on a twofold base of the trochaic septenarius (seven complete feet and an additional syllable or "half-foot" at the end of each line) and iambic senarius (six complete iambic feet), but handles this pattern with a liberal use of substitution and with an ear for easy and flowing movement.

The lyric songs, in quite different meters, constitute a reworking of the earlier pattern of lyrics in the Greek drama, which had fallen into disuse and are now reintroduced for change of mood and pace. The "song" of either Désirée or Messenio, for example, changes and brightens the scene, momentarily clearing it of the mounting complications of the plot. The intricate metrical structure shows Latin at its most extended power of rhythmic variety, just as the vocabulary and alliterative diction show Latin at an exuberant, flamboyant phase, not unlike the fecundity and verve we can sense in Renaissance English writing. As for the "one-man" chorus, or song-and-dance routine, made possible by the lyric song passages, it should be said that the derivation is from the native Italian as well as the traditional Greek. The chanting buoyance and sprightly meters of these songs owe much to the native country balladry and folksong indigenous to the Italian peasants, the Fescennine spirit that preceded the literary arts of comedy and satire. The comedy of Plautus seems to have drawn its inspiration from many different sources, reflecting in temper the bright outlook for a hopeful future, directly incorporating major elements from the traditional Greek reservoir of dramatic models and aesthetic practices, while reshaping these into a new medium in a new language, and stemming from the native Fescennine raillery and folk poetry written in the Saturnian accentual scheme.

Of as much importance in studying Plautus as the intellectual implications of plot and thought or the specialized techniques of verse composition is the simple matter of his comic attitude. It is readily enough seen that *The Menaechmi* abounds in farce and a kind of hard-headed "fun" which Plautus lets loose on the stage at will. Obviously he means for us to laugh at the predicaments and roar at the characters, not sympathize with them. It is a hard world, he seems to say, and we might as well try to make the most of it and land on our feet if possible. It is a hard world for Désirée and Peniculus, for example; the cliff-hanging statusless woman and the insolvent man-about-town must brazen their way through and manipulate realistically to survive. Furthermore, love affairs are all very well, but they take more money than they are worth. It is a hard world for the indispensable slave, whose gifts and energies sometimes encourage us to laugh with him and at his master. The free and easygoing young men of substance command our interest if not our respect by their near imperturbability. Like the "dramatic street" on which Roman comedy is played with its stage one hundred and eighty feet long, its standard backdrop of two houses, two exit streets (one leading to the forum, the other to the harbor or country), and its alley for eavesdropping, the comic situation represents a rather open and matter-of-fact way of life. The psychology of its action affords few occasions for soul-searching or remorse, and its busy conduct leads directly to sudden laughter or startled dismay.

Still, there is room for criticism, wry analysis, and considerable, if impulsive and exaggerated, emotional involvement. Peniculus's oration against public orations, Menaechmus I's full cry against the commercial entanglements of the legal process—both touch on sensitive areas of Roman sociology. Messenio's successes and the perplexed, unsuitable wife's failures evoke some measure of sympathy, whereas the dense doctor and the hard girlfriend evoke little. Perhaps the most appealing character in this play is the old father-in-law, canny and clear-minded; debilitated as he appears, he makes a most experienced authority on old age. Thrown together in this tough outdoor world, Plautus's band of characters carom off one another, unleashing lines of witty abuse and artful conciliation, bending their whole energies to the solution of a situation that is perfectly real and graspable, and wildly incongruous.

Although there are several passages and lines open to various interpretations, I have not added notes to my translation because the technical consideration of all disputed points is available in the scholarly editions of the play.

In translating into English verse I have relied on a flexible version of the iambic pentameter as the fundamental line rhythm for dialogue where Plautus uses the septenarius or senarius. While trying to preserve the main stress of five beats a line, I have expanded the number of syllables beyond the ten used in strict iambic pentameter, and have occasionally extended the line to a hexameter. I employ rhyme as well, in the hope of registering an English equivalent for Plautus's anaphora, assonance, and alliteration. Plautus's sound effects have encouraged me to try freely for rhyme sounds—initial, medial, and end rhymes—as a means of imitating to some degree the explosive sonority of his amazing ear-filling Latin. I change from rhyme to blank verse and return to rhyme, for the purpose of breaking the monotony of one metrical style. In the lyric passages I have used shorter lines and different rhyme forms in an effort to imitate the lyric shape of the original Latin. Throughout the translation I have tried to reproduce as clearly as I could the temper and spirit of Plautus's comedy wherein, for all the carefree writing and abandonment of exposition to the farcical moment, there persists a steady and generous supply of good humor and good sense.

PALMER BOVIE

Indiana University

The Menaechmi

PENICULUS [Brush], a parasite

MENAECHMUS I, a young gentleman living in Epidamnus

MENAECHMUS II [Sosicles], a young gentleman of Syracuse

DÉSIRÉE [Erotium], a courtesan

MIXMASTER [Cylindrus], her cook

MESSENIO, slave of MENAECHMUS II [Sosicles]

MAID, in the service of DÉSIRÉE

WIFE, wife of MENAECHMUS I

OLD MAN, father-in-law of MENAECHMUS I

A DOCTOR

WHIPSTER I

WHIPSTER II

PROLOGUS IN PERSON

Ladies and gentlemen, and everybody else, I announce
In the first fine foremost and friendly words I pronounce,
Myself! How are you all out there? Do let me greet you.
It's a particular pride and personal privilege to meet you,
And present to you Plautus in person, that is as he looks
When he speaks in his very own words; I don't mean in books
Where you read what he says, but here on the stage where he *is*.
Won't you lend us your ears and put yourselves quite at ease,
Tune in on our logic, and turn your minds to the plot
I now go over in a very few words, not a lot?
        Oh yes . . . poets often insist, more often than not
In their comedies, "It's an action in Athens," it takes place
Where you're expected to find it most charming, in Greece. [*Irish
    pronunciation*]
        But I'm not the underhanded sort who is willing to say
It takes place somewhere it doesn't, or . . . anyway
Nowhere except *when* it does occur there. And today
While I grant that our play bubbles up through Greek grounds,
It's distilled in Sicilian, not acted in Attic towns.
So your Prologue expounds the preface to his foreword. He pounds
In the plot now, not a little, but a lot; it's scoops of synopsis
To ladle out. I'll shovel on now, and bury my worries,
In view of the generous way you hear out our stories.
        A certain old man was a merchant in Syracuse.
To him twin sons were born, identical youths
So alike in appearance the wet nurse could never get used
To telling them apart when she popped up to offer her breasts;
Their own mother didn't know which was which, she just guessed.
Well . . . at least, that's what someone who saw these boys once
    told me:
I don't want you thinking *I* went there and saw them, you see.
Now one day when both boys were seven, their father loaded up
A huge cargo ship full of goods to be sold, and toted up
One of the boys on the boat. Then off they went
To the market together being held in the town of Tarentum;
The other son, of course, he left back home with the mother.
And when they got to Tarentum, the father and the other,
There was some sort of fair going on, with hundreds of games,
And hundreds of people to watch them, which quickly explains
How the boy wandered off in the crowd, away from his dad.
A merchant from Epidamnus latched on to the lad

3

And snatched him off home. And then when the father discovered
He'd lost his son, sick at heart, he never recovered
From the fatal depression that carried him right to his grave
In Tarentum a few days later on. When the messenger arrived
At Syracuse with this grisly news of how the father lay dead
At Tarentum, and twin number one was completely mislaid,
The affectionate grandfather promptly took it in his head
To rename the Syracuse son in honor of the other,
And call him Menaechmus from now on, after his brother;
So dear to the grandfather's heart was that boy and his name:
The grandfather's own, as a matter of fact, was the same.
I remember that name *Menaechmus* all right, all the better
Because I'm sure I've seen it stuck up somewhere in *Big Letters*.
Isn't that just like us? "Hmmm, *Menaechmus* . . ." we say,
Funny how it strikes us . . . "Haven't I seen that somewhere to-
    day?"
But, not to lead you astray,
I hereby officially announce, pronounce, and relay
The fact that both twins henceforth have identical names.
    Now, my feet must head Epidamnuswards, for the claims
Of this complicated plot I must measure by the foot; this explains,
I hope, how metricalloused my rhythmic diet may be.
To survey this plot I must personally run on and see
Where it happens to be ambling along itself, iambically.
And if any of you out there have something you'd like me to do
At Epidamnus for you, speak up and let me know.
Don't forget what things cost, though; I'll need some dough.
If you don't tip you're bound to be rooked, even though
When you do tip you'll also be had, for the money will flow
Even farther; the less you hold on to, the more you let go.
    Anyway, here I am back where I started. I stand as
I orginally did when I came out and ran on. Epidamnus
Is the name of the place, you remember the merchant of which
Kidnaped the twin other brother. Being very rich,
But childless, he adopted the boy to add interest to his life,
And invested as well for his son in a suitable wife
With a juicy dowry, to marry, and arranged his whole life
By making Menaechmus his heir, when he passed away.
Not bad for a lad whose dad was a thief, wouldn't you say?
And curiously enough, that end came around rather soon;
For the merchant was out in the country, not far from town
On a day it had rained very hard, and started across a river.
Darned if that body-snatching sliver of a river didn't deliver
The kidnaper himself into the hands of his jailer forever,
And clap the chap off the scene in death's unseen trap.
Menaechmus promptly inherited a fortune; although kidnaped,

He is very well off in Epidamnus. He feels quite at ease
And at home with his funds. And guess now, just who would breeze
Into town just today with his slave on the run right behind him?
Menaechmus (~~you like this~~?) to search for his brother, and find him
Perhaps . . . we'll see about that. *Twins Billed to Appear*
At Epidamnus today. Of course, they wouldn't be here
Not a bit of it, if our plot didn't admit of it, but *there*
Wherever the story demanded, and in that case I'd steer
You to the right destination and make the situation clear.

In the acting profession things tend to change: the town
The play's in, the actor's part, the lines handed down
He has to say. That house front behind me, for instance,
Depends for its very existence on the playwright's insistence
In installing inside it the characters he would provide it
With, and let live a moment; not even reside, it
Appears, but multiply or divide there. Shifty as the truth,
It houses an oldster, kings, beggars, gangsters, a youth;
A sharp-witted bellyaching sponger, any kind of quack
You can think of, the real one, the fake. Our profession is kind,
And makes room for all. Like me, the actors will remind
You of the double dealings dwelling anon in our comedy.
I'm off and away now, just going down on one knee
To hope you'll applaud us: smile on poor Plautus
   And Not Frown on Me!

ACT ONE

Scene One

[PENICULUS]

PENICULUS The boys all call me Peniculus, which may sound
    ridiculous
    But just means *Table Duster* and shows *How Able an Adjuster*
    I am to dinner and meticulous in clearing off the table:
    You can call me Soft Hairbrush: It seems to be my fate
    To be famous as a famished feaster and wear such a tail plate.
        You know, some men chain down their captives, and they
            shackle
    The legs of runaway slaves. I think *that's* ridiculous,
    To load still worse weight on a badly enough burdened crate.
    If you put pressure on him, the underdog *wants* to get up
    And take off, and never do another stroke of work.
    Somehow, they'll always wriggle loose, file off the link
    Or knock the lock to bits with a rock. Are chains worth the pains?
    If you'd like to rope someone in, so he doesn't feel
    Like escaping, snare him with wine and a meal!
    You're putting a ring through his nose when you take him to
        dinner.
    And as long as you keep him well stocked with food and liquor,
    Regularly and the way he likes it, he'll stick with you,
    Even though he's under heavy sentence. He'll want to serve you;
    As long as you're bound to give him food, he's bound to eat it.
    The nets and meshes of food are remarkably strong
    And elastic, and squeeze even tighter when they get long.
    I'm off to Menaechmus' at the moment, where I've signed on
    To appear for dinner. I volunteer gaily for a jail
    Like his, especially at meals. He doesn't feed, he deals
    With his guests, increasing their status; like a good restauranteur
    He doesn't diagnose, he offers a cure. This sharp epicure
    Puts out a very fine spread, he doesn't spare the courses;
    He builds up skyscrapers of dishes—you see something delicious
    And have to stand up on the couch and stretch out to reach it
    Over all the other things that look nearly as luscious.
    I've been out of commission for quite a long intermission,
    Not in the preferred position at Menaechmus' house, but at home,
    Domiciled and dominated by my own little sweetmeats. Those
        treats

6

I provide for myself and my near ones have proved dear ones,
Thanks to my expensive tastes—and they all go to waist.
So I'm drumming myself out of those ranks, not burning up money
Trooping in with food for the group. Instead, I'm turning tummy
To Menaechmus' place. He may just embrace my company. Here
   he comes now
Flouncing out of the house—looks like they've had a row.

Scene Two

[PENICULUS and MENAECHMUS I]

MENAECHMUS I   If you weren't such a mean, prying snoop,
   You stoop, you'd see that when I blow up
   It's *your* fault. You'd better stop, or
   I'll pack you right back to your papa,
   Drooping out-of-doors, divorced, good and proper.
           Every time I go for a walk, you let go a squawk
   And assault me with questions. Where am I going?
   What's doing? Where? What's *that* I've got there?
   I didn't bring home a wife, I brought home a hawk-
   Eyed customs inspector, an unconscientious objector
   To everything I do. One who makes me *declare*
   Everything I've got in mind. Oh woemankind!
   Personal effects, you defect detective. Oh, the heck with it!
   I guess I've spoiled you with too much attention
   And turned this into a house of detention.
   From now on, things will be different. I'm here to mention
   What I expect or else from your lie detector: shelves full of
      silence;
   No more prying, my high-powered Highness; absolute, utter
      compliance.
   I gave you money and clothes,
   Robes and dresses, domestics;
   I've been pretty good and elastic
   In meeting your demands.
   You keep your hands, and your nose,
   Out of my business. That's the best trick
   To play if you want to stay on good terms with me.
   Why look over, inspect, and go right on shaking
   The man who's made you a major in his own homemaking?
   To prove that you can't fence me in, I've promised today
   To take a girl out to dinner and reward you that way.

PENICULUS   Taking it out on his wife? Taking that line
   Won't ruin his wife but will leave me out on a limb.

MENAECHMUS I Ah now, by God, and good show! I've finally
   told my wife where to go:
Inside, and to leave me alone. Now where are you uxorious types,
   all of you
Out there, you who ought to be oozing up front to shower your
   thanks
On me for fighting the good fight? And look what I've done,
   each and every one
Of you, my fellow sufferers. I've taken this delicate mantilla-dress
Out of my wife's most favorite chest, to present to my girl.
An excellent trick, don't you think, to reward the warden
By stealing something right from under her nose? I propose
A subject for congratulations: this beautifully planned,
Charming little crime, dutifully and well carried out:
Converting a legalized loss to a preferable self-ruination.
Diverting the loot from the foe's hands to those of our allies.

PENICULUS I say there, young fellow, what share in the prize can I
   Hope to realize?

MENAECHMUS I God! I've dropped into a trap!

PENICULUS Not at all, a fortified position.

MENAECHMUS I   Who in perdition
   Are you?

PENICULUS Fine, thanks, who are you? I'm me, as a matter of
   fact.

MENAECHMUS I Oh, you. My most modern convenience, you
   beautifully timed supergadget!

PENICULUS Greetings.

MENAECHMUS I   What are you doing at the moment?

PENICULUS   Fervently latching
   Onto the hand of my right-hand man.

MENAECHMUS I   You couldn't be stringing along
   At a better time than this that's bringing you on into my orbit.

PENICULUS That's how I usually time my launching forth in search
   of a luncheon.
I've studied, got the thing down pat, I don't just play my hunches.

MENAECHMUS I Want to feast your eyes on a sparkling treat I've
   completed
The arrangements for?

PENICULUS   It'll look less crooked to me when I see
   Who's cooked it up. If there's been any slip-up in preparing this
   fête

I'll know when I see what's left untouched on the plate.

MENAECHMUS I   Say, you've seen the famous painting plastered against a wall
Showing the eagle ferrying off that handsome sort of fancy-bred boyfriend
To his handler in the sky? Or the one that shows Venus' and Adonis'
Bare . . . ?

PENICULUS   Kneeness? Sure, lots of times, but what do I care about art?

MENAECHMUS I   Just look at me? Don't I do that part to perfection?

PENICULUS   Cahn't sigh I'm accustomed to a costume . . . what the hell is that you're wearing?

MENAECHMUS   Aren't I the apple of your eye, your Prince Charming? Come on, say it.

PENICULUS   Not until I know what time dinner is and whether I'm invited.

MENAECHMUS I   Why not be so disarming as to admit what I ask you to?

PENICULUS   All right, all right, Prince, you're charming.

MENAECHMUS I   Anything else
You'd like to add voluntarily?

PENICULUS   Well, that's a fairly airily merrily
Wingspread you've got there.

MENAECHMUS I   More, more! Makes me *soar!*

PENICULUS   Damned if I'll say any more, by God in heaven, until I get some whiff
Of what my reward will be if. You've had a row with your wife.
I'd better look out warily carefully, my life is in danger.

MENAECHMUS I   Incidentally, my wife hasn't a clue about where we're going, to do
The town today. We're going to set the hot spots on fire.

PENICULUS   Well, thank heavens, now you make sense. How soon do I light the pyre?
The day's half used up already, dead down to the navel.

MENAECHMUS I   You're slowing up the show, interrupting with that drivel.

PENICULUS   Knock out my eye, Menaechmus, dig it into the ground, bash it

Back and below till it comes out my ankle, if I ever make a sound
From now on, except to say what you order me to.

MENAECHMUS I Just step over here, away from my door.

PENICULUS How's this for size?

MENAECHMUS I A little farther, please.

PENICULUS It's a breeze. How's this? Far enough?

MENAECHMUS I Now, step out, like a man safe out of reach of
the lion's den.

PENICULUS By God in heaven, if you wouldn't make the best
jockey.

MENAECHMUS I How come?

PENICULUS You keep looking back over your shoulder to see
If your wife isn't thudding up behind you.

MENAECHMUS I You're telling me?

PENICULUS I'm telling you? Well, fellow, I'm not telling you any-
thing,
Let's get that clear; just what you want to hear, or you don't.
That much I'll say, or I won't. I'm your best yes man yet.

MENAECHMUS I All right, let's have a guess, then, at what you
can make of
This garment I'm exposing to your nose. What sort oi scent
Does it put you on the trail of . . . ? Why get pale and shove it
out of range?

PENICULUS Strange, it doesn't put me on the trail of, it pins me
to the tail of . . .
Look here, old boy, you know as well as I do, men shouldn't
try to
Imbibe the fragrance of feminine apparel except from up near
the top
Of same dainty. Down lower the unwashed part makes you feel
fainty.

MENAECHMUS I All right, Peniculus, try this part over here; tickle
your nose
With this wholesome whiff. Aha! Now you make like truffles.

PENICULUS Sure, it suits my snuffles.

MENAECHMUS I Oh, puffle, come on and say,
Say what it tells you. What sort of smells you deduce.

PENICULUS Phew, what a naral escape! I'm glad to produce my
solution.
This is my diagnosis: You steal a *jeune fille* for a meal;

You purloin a *fräulein* for some sirloin; you flirt with a skirt
And alert your tastebuds to a smorgasbord; a distress
And theft, and this dress is left for your mistress to drape round
Her; gleaming napery; conjugal japery, all very vapory. The
    whole deal,
From my point of view, leads straight toward an excellent meal,
    and I'm joining you.

MENAECHMUS I   Don't! I'm not coming apart. But you've hit
The female suggestion on the head, no question, and orated
    convincingly.
For I've pretty winsomely sneaked this dress from my wife
And am spiriting it off to the niftiest mistress of mine,
Désirée. I'm ordering a banquet, this very day
For you and me, a treat at her place.

PENICULUS   Oh, I say!

MENAECHMUS I   We'll drink from now till tomorrow's morning
    star puts out
This night so bibulous.

PENICULUS   I say, you *are* fabulous. Shall I knock
At Désirée's door?

MENAECHMUS I   Sure, go ahead. No, better knock off.
Hold it! I said.

PENICULUS   You're the one that's holding it: my head
Wants to get at that bottle, not back off a mile in the distance.

MENAECHMUS I   Knock very gently.

PENICULUS   The door, evidently, 's the consistency
Of papyrus.

MENAECHMUS I   Knock off, I insist, do desist! God in heaven!
Lay off or I'll knock your block off! And besides, rub your eyes:
Can't you see? Here she comes out, herself, free and easy. Her
    body
Eclipses the sun. An excellent exit, dancing
Into view like this; she wins more acclaim than the flame
Of the sun. He goes quite blind, when I find her so entrancing.

Scene Three

[DÉSIRÉE, PENICULUS, *and* MENAECHMUS I]

DÉSIRÉE   Oh, my dear, *dear* Menaechmus, how *are* you today?

PENICULUS   Hey, say!
What about me? Don't I rate a greeting?

DÉSIRÉE   Zero, you cipher.

PENICULUS Well, a soldier has to get used to being a serial number, I guess.

MENAECHMUS I Now darling look here, I would love to have you
go and fix up . . .

PENICULUS Ohhh, fray can you see? Let's have us a mix-up: you
be the smorgas
And I'll come aboard you. We'll fight it out all day; ohhh, I
say . . .
Till the dawn's early light, which of us battlers is the heavier
weight
When it comes to hitting the bottle. Daisy, you can be the
general,
And feel free to choose which company you'll spend the duration
Of this dark operation with. Let's hope your proper ration is
. . . me.

MENAECHMUS I Sweet and lovely! How loathly my wife appears
in my eyes
When they light on you.

PENICULUS   Meanwhile you put on her things
And wifey still clings to you.

DÉSIRÉE   What in the world . . . ?

MENAECHMUS I   I'm unfurled.
My dear girl. Here's the dress I deprive my wife of and provide
You with. You look better in her clothes than she does without
them,
My rose.

DÉSIRÉE Touché or not touché, I must say I must give way
To so super-sartorial an assault on my virtue. You win the day.

PENICULUS Listen to the mistress whisper sweet somethings, as
long as
She sees he's bringing her that gay thing for nothing. Now is
The time, if you love her, to have what you want of her
In the form of some toothsome kisses.

MENAECHMUS I   Oh, hang up, Brush Face.
I've only done just what I swore I would with this garment:
placed
It on the altar of her grace.

PENICULUS   By God in heaven, I give in!

Listen, *twist* in it, won't you? I can see you in the ballet, like a
fine
Boy, a dear for the dance, with the veil trailing behind your
tight pants.

MENAECHMUS I   Dance, me? By God in heaven, you're crazy.

PENICULUS   Me, crazy?
I'd say, easy does it, *you* may be *that* way instead, in your head.

DÉSIRÉE   If you're not going to wear it, take it off then. And stop
saying
"By God in heaven!"

MENAECHMUS I   After all I won this today by playing a
A pretty dangerous game; I stole it.

PENICULUS   On the whole, it's even more fraying
To the nerves than Hercules (or "heavenly God," if you please)
Swerving round those curves to steal Hippolyta's girdle and sneak
off swaying.
I'd say you were in more mortal danger than that thievish
stranger
Ever ran into, even though he was stronger.

MENAECHMUS I   I can no longer
Hold back this offer I proffer to you, Désirée. So do have it,
You wonderful girl, sole creature alive sympathetic to my wants.

DÉSIRÉE   This is the true-hearted sort of fervor nature should
always transplant
In the souls of romancers whose desires are their favorite haunts.

PENICULUS   Or at least sharp sparks going broke at full speed
chasing spooks.

MENAECHMUS I   I bought it for my wife last year. $85.00.

PENICULUS   We can close the books on that sum and kiss it
good-by.

MENAECHMUS I   And now can you guess what I want to do?

DÉSIRÉE   Yes, I know
And what's more I'll do what you want.

MENAECHMUS I   Dinner for three,
Chez Daisy. Order this done and I'll be pleased.

PENICULUS   And say, see
While you're at it that whoever goes to buy the food at the forum
Picks out something specially tasty; a perfect little pork filet
Or savory thin-sliced prosciutto, ham recherché,
Like a succulent half-section head of a pig—let's do it the big
way,

And have that ham so well cooked that I can pounce on the table
like a hawk
Who knows what he likes, and then strikes. And let's make it
quick.

DÉSIRÉE   By Jiminy, yes! You're on!

MENAECHMUS I   That's very nice, the way you didn't
Say "By God in heaven." Me and old slothful here, we're head-
ing down-
Town to hang around the forum and see what's up. We'll be right
back.
While dinner's cooking, we'll start with the drinking.

DÉSIRÉE   Come on
Along whenever you want. Things will be ready.

MENAECHMUS I   But do get a steady move on.
Now let's go, and let's you keep up.

PENICULUS   By God in heaven, how true!
I'll follow you all right and I'll slave for you too. If I lost you
Today and got all the wealth in heaven, I wouldn't break even.

[*Exeunt* MENAECHMUS I *and* PENICULUS.]

DÉSIRÉE [*alone*]   I wonder why they always say "God in heaven"?
Where else could he be?
You, girls in there! Call out Mixmaster, the head cook,
And tell him to come outside here. I need him this minute.

[*Enter* MIXMASTER.]

DÉSIRÉE   Take this shopping basket, my man, and, yes, here's
some money;
Let's see . . . $9.63.

MIXMASTER   Right you are, miss.

DÉSIRÉE   Now scoot, Sonny-boy
And get on with your catering. Buy enough for three people
only,
No more, no less.

MIXMASTER   Who's coming?

DÉSIRÉE   Menaechmus, and that lonely
Crowd of his, Soft Hair, the never-to-be-brushed off, plus me.

MIXMASTER   Well, Miss, that's three *times* three plus one, actually:
Peniculus eats enough for eight, and you both make two.

DÉSIRÉE   I've given out the guest list. The rest of this is up to you.

MIXMASTER   Right you are, Miss. The dinner is as good as all
done.
You can all take your places. Won't you all please sit down?

DÉSIRÉE   Get going now, you fix-faster, and hurry right back from
town.

MIXMASTER   I'll be back here so soon you won't even know I've
been gone.

ACT TWO

Scene One

[MENAECHMUS II *and* MESSENIO]

MENAECHMUS II   Messenio, I tell you, there's no greater source
   of delight
   For sailors than to look out across the deep water and sight
   The land they're heading for.

MESSENIO   I couldn't be more
   In agreement, provided the land you refer to is home. Therefore,
   Why in hell, I implore you, are *we* in Epidamnus?
   Do you plan to act like the ocean and noisily slam us
   Against every damned piece of land we can touch?

MENAECHMUS II   As much
   As I need to cover to locate my own twin, my brother.

MESSENIO   But how much longer do we have to keep looking for
   him?
   It's six years now since we started. When we departed
   You didn't say we'd try everywhere, moseying to Marseilles,
   Skirting around Spain, bounding back to menace Venice,
   And do the whole coastal *bit* from Trieste to Dubrovnik to Split,
   Or skim the whole rim of Italy, littorally. As the sea
   Goes, that's where we rows. My point is—a haystack
   With the well-known needle in it . . . you'd have found it. But
   we lack
   The object to bring our search to a head. He's quite dead,
   The man you're after, while you ransack the land of the living
   If he were anywhere around you'd have found him.

MENAECHMUS II   I won't give in
   Until I've found out for sure from someone I have to believe in
   Who'll say that he knows that my brother is dead. And when that
   day
   Arrives, our travels are over. But I *won't* stop pursuing
   My other half, and I know what I'm doing: he means
   Everything to me.

MESSENIO   You're looking for a knot in a marshmallow
   reed.
   We won't go home until we've gone round the world, then, as
   fellow
   Travelers, and written a book about what it looks like?

16

MENAECHMUS II   I doubt it.
But see here, my boy, you just do as you're told; don't be too
  bold;
Eat your food; be good; don't be a bother. It's not your good
That matters in this expedition.

MESSENIO   Take that definition
Of a typical slave's condition. I know who I am now, all right.
He couldn't have put a bigger proposition in many fewer words,
Or in so clear a light. Still and all, I just can't keep stalling
Around; I can't just stop talking. You listening, Menaechmus?
My purse, I mean, our purse, now that I look at it,
Has too much vacation space; our wardrobe there looks quite
  scanty,
Are we going in for summer sports? By God in heaven, you'll
  groan,
Exhausted by the search for your twin, unless you turn back
  home.
They'll *wham* us in Epidamnus, positive; Dubrovnik us to clink-
  ers.
The town's chock full of nuts, fast-living long-range drinkers,
Go-between wheedlers, middlemen who take you, the stinkers,
In to be cleaned and doused by the masters of the house,
I mean mistresses, who whisper sweet slopniks to you,
And profit from your losses in the process. That's what they do,
Damn us strangers in this town. No wonder it's called, up and
  down,
Epidamnus; every damn one of us innocents in Greece
Gets introduced here to the golden fleece, before he's released,
Enormously decreased in value.

MENAECHMUS II   Take it easy. Hand me that greasy
Wallet.

MESSENIO   What do you want with it?

MENAECHMUS II   Your speech has haunted
Me. I'm panicked by your frantic appeal to the facts of life.

MESSENIO   Afraid, why afraid for me? . . .

MENAECHMUS II   You'll whammy us both in Epidamnus.
You're a great lady's man, Messenio: I know you. And I?
I'm a man of many moods, all of which prompt me to fly
Off the handle in a hurry. And since I'm the furious sort,
And you the luxurious sport, always in pursuit of a skirt,
I'll manage both crises nicely, and simply divert
The money into my control. Then you won't waste the whole

Thing on women; and I won't get mad when you do; or even peeved.

MESSENIO Take it and keep it then, do. I'm somewhat relieved.

Scene Two

[MIXMASTER, MENAECHMUS II, *and* MESSENIO]

MIXMASTER I've shopped very shrewdly and well, if I say so myself:
I'll spread a fine feast in front of these dauntless diners.
Oh, oh, Menaechmus, already! I'll bet I'm in for a beating:
The guests have arrived and here I've just gotten back
From the market. They're walking around in front of the house;
I'll go up and greet them. Menaechmus, good afternoon!

MENAECHMUS II Best wishes, old chap, whoever you happen to be.

MIXMASTER Whoever I'm . . . ? You don't say, Menaechmus, you don't know?

MENAECHMUS II Oh God in heaven, you know I don't.

MIXMASTER   But where
Are the rest of our guests?

MENAECHMUS II   What guests?

MIXMASTER   Your parasite, for one.

MENAECHMUS II My parasite? Obviously this fellow is quite off his nut.

MESSENIO Didn't I tell you this town was lousy with scroungers?

MENAECHMUS II Which parasite of mine did you mean, young man?

MIXMASTER Why that peachy little Peniculus, the fuzzy table duster.

MESSENIO Oh *him,* peenie brush? He's safe all right, here in our bag.

MIXMASTER Menaechmus, you've come along a bit soon for dinner:
I'm just getting back from buying the food.

MENAECHMUS II   Listen here,
How much does a good box of sure-fire tranquilizers cost
In this town?

MIXMASTER $1.98 for the economy size.

MENAECHMUS II Here's $3.96. Get yourself a double prescription.
I can see you're quite out of control, making trouble like this
For someone like me you don't even know, whoever *you* are.

MIXMASTER I'm Mixmaster: that's not complicated, and don't
say you don't know it.

MENAECHMUS II You can be Mixmaster, or Sizzling Ham Steak
With Cloves En Brochette,
I couldn't care less. I've never seen you before today
And now that I have, I'm not at all very pleased to meet you.

MIXMASTER Your name's Menaechmus.

MENAECHMUS II   You seem to be talking sense
At the moment, since you call me by name, but where did you
learn
Who I am?

MIXMASTER Who you are? When I work for your mistress right
in this house?
Désirée?

MENAECHMUS II By God, she's *not* my mistress and I *do not*
Know you.

MIXMASTER Don't know *me,* who pours you out drink after drink
when you come here
For dinner?

MESSENIO   I wish I could lay hands on something to bat this
nut with.

MENAECHMUS II *You* mix drinks and pour them for *me,* for *me,*
Who never even came this way, much less saw Epidamnus
Before today?

MIXMASTER   Never even saw it, you say?

MENAECHMUS II Yes; I mean *no,* dear God in heaven, so help
me, *no!*

MIXMASTER I suppose you don't really live in that house over
there?

MENAECHMUS II May the gods cave the roof in hard on whoever
does!

MIXMASTER Stark, raving loony. Wishing himself such bad luck.
Can you hear me, Menaechmus?

MENAECHMUS II   Depends on what you're saying.

MIXMASTER Now look, take my advice. Remember that $3.96
You offered to give me a minute ago for the pills?
Go spend it on yourself; you're the one who needs it the most,

And the soonest, calling down curses, by God in heaven,
On your very own head. You're just not *all there,* Menaechmus.
If you've any brains left you'll send out at once for the medicine;
There's a new triple dose thing out, The Three Little Big Tran-
quilizers,
Frightens off all kinds of weird wolves.

MENAECHMUS II   He sure talks a lot.

MIXMASTER   Of course, Menaechmus always teases me, like this;
he's a joker
When his wife's not around. What's that you're saying Menaechmus?

MENAECHMUS II   I beg your pardon, Mixmaster, did you say
something?

MIXMASTER   How does this stuff look? Like enough for dinner for
three?
Or shall I go out and buy more for the girlfriend and you
And your parasite pal?

MENAECHMUS II   Women? Parasite? Pals? What women,
what parasites, pal?

MESSENIO   Look here, old boy, what terrible crime is weighing on
your mind
And making you pester him so?

MIXMASTER   Stranger boy, you stay out
Of my business; I'll conduct that with the person I know
And am talking to.

MESSENIO   Oh God in . . . I give up; except for the fact
That I'm sure as can be that this cook is completely cracked.

MIXMASTER   Well, now, I'll just get busy with these things. I can
promise you
Some succulent results, very soon. You'll stay around the house,
Menaechmus, I hope. Anything else you can think of?

MENAECHMUS II   I can think of you as one real upside-down
cake. You're baked.

MIXMASTER   Oh by God in . . . somewhere or other, I could
swear it's you
Who are the mixed-up master. I wish you would go . . . lie down
Somewhere until you feel better, while I take this stuff
And commit it to the fire-breathing forces of Vulcan. I'll tell
Désirée you're out here. She'll want to ask you in, I feel sure.

[*goes into the house*]

MENAECHMUS II Gone, has he? God, how right I see your words
were
When you talked about this place.

MESSENIO   Mark my words further.
One of those fast working, loose-jointed women lives here, you
can bet,
As sure as that crackpot cook who went in there said she did.

MENAECHMUS II I do wonder, though, how he came by my
name?

MESSENIO That's easy.
Why, that's a cinch. The women have it all worked out.
They send their slave boys or housemaids down to the docks.
When a strange ship comes in, they ask the passenger's name,
And find out where he's from. Later on, they pick him up cas-
ually
And stick close to him. If their charms have the right effect
They ship him back home plucked quite clean of his money.

[*pointing to Désirée's house*]

And right over there rocks a fast little pirate sloop at anchor:
We'd better look out for her, and look sharp, Commander.

MENAECHMUS II Damned if I don't think you're right.

MESSENIO   I'll know what you think
For sure when I see what preeeeecautions you're taking.

MENAECHMUS II   Just a moment.
I hear the door swinging open; let's see who comes out.

MESSENIO I'll drop our seabag right here. Heave ho, my bellboys!
You fleet runners, shift this gear into neutral for a while.

Scene Three

[DÉSIRÉE, MENAECHMUS II, *and* MESSENIO]

DÉSIRÉE [*singing gaily*] Open the doors, open wide: I don't want
them shut.
You in there, look to it, come here and do it,
What has to be done:
Couches to be hung with fine drapes;
Tables adorned; some incense burned;
Lights set blazing; the place made amazing.

To dazzle and delight your bright lover's heart
Is to play with skill your gay charming part,
And importune at his expense while you make your fortune.
    Where is he though? A moment ago, my cook said I'd find
      him standing
Around by the door . . . oh there he is, the one I adore when
  he's handing
His money over freely. I'll ask him in now for the meal he
  wanted made ready
And get him started on the drinks, to keep him from staying too
  steady.
I'll just slip over and speak to him first.
Oh my favorite fellow, my poor heart will burst
If you keep standing here outside
When the doors to our house are open wide
To take you in. It's much more your place,
This house, than your own home is, an embrace,
A bright smile on its face just for you, and a kiss
On that most generous of mouths. This really is your house.
And now all is prepared just the way you wanted
And shortly we'll serve you your dinner and pour out the wine.

    [*pause*]

I said, the meal's all in order, just as you commanded;
Whenever you're ready, come on in now, honey, any time.

MENAECHMUS II Who in the world does this woman think she's
  talking to?

DÉSIRÉE To you, that's who.

MENAECHMUS II   But what business have I with you
At present, or what have I ever had to do with you up to now?

DÉSIRÉE Heavens! It's you that Venus has inspired me to prize
Over all the others, and you've certainly turned out to be worth it.
Heavens above! You've set me up high enough with your gen-
  erous gifts!

MENAECHMUS II This woman is surely quite crazy or definitely
  drunk,
Messenio, talking such intimate stuff to me
A man she doesn't even know.

MESSENIO   I told you so!
And now, it's only the leaves that are falling, just wait;
Spend three more days in this town and the trees themselves
Will be crashing down down on your head. The women are
  biased,

Buy us this, buy us that, and buzzing around for your money.
But let me talk to her. Hey, sweetie, I'm speaking to you.

DÉSIRÉE You're what?

MESSENIO   No, I'm not, I'm who. And while I'm at it,
just *where*
Did you get to know the man here who's with me so well?

DÉSIRÉE Why, right here in Epidamnus, where I've been for so
long.

MESSENIO Epidamnus? A place he never set foot in before today?

DÉSIRÉE A *delicious* joke, you rascal. Now, Menaechmus, darling,
Won't you come in? You'll feel much cozier and settled.

MENAECHMUS II By God, the woman's quite right to call me by
my own name.
Still I can't help wondering what's up.

MESSENIO   She's got wind of your moneybag,
The one you relieved me of.

MENAECHMUS II   And damned if you didn't alert me
To that very thing. Here, you'd better take it. That way,
I can find out for sure whether she's after me, or my money.

DÉSIRÉE *Andiam', O caro bene!* And we'll tuck right into that
meal;
Mangiamo, igitur, et cetera.

MENAECHMUS II   Music to my ears,
And you're very nice to sing it, my dear. I only regret
I cannot accept.

DÉSIRÉE   But why in the world did you tell me, a short
while ago,
To have dinner ready for you?

MENAECHMUS II   *I* told *you* to have dinner ready?

DÉSIRÉE Of course, dinner for three, you, your parasite, and me.

MENAECHMUS II Oh hell, lady, what the hell is all this parasite
stuff?
God, what a woman! She's crazy as can be once again.

DÉSIRÉE Cookie duster Peniculus, C. D. Peniculus, the crumb
devourer.

MENAECHMUS II But I mean what kind of a peniculus? We all
know that's a soft hair
Brush, but I don't know anyone *named* that. You mean my ri-
diculous

Little thing, the traveling shoebrush I carry for my suede sandals,
The better to buff them with? What peniculus hangs so close
to me?

DÉSIRÉE You know I mean that local leech who just now came
by with you
When you brought me that sweet silk dress you stole from your
wife.

MENAECHMUS II I gave you a dress, did I? One I stole from my
wife?
You're sure? I'd swear you were asleep, like a horse standing up.

DÉSIRÉE Oh gosh, what's the fun of making fun of me and denying
Everything you've done?

MENAECHMUS II   Just tell me what I'm denying.

DÉSIRÉE That you gave me today your wife's most expensive silk
dress.

MENAECHMUS II All right, I deny that. I'm not married. And I've
never been married.
And I've never come near this port since the day I was born,
Much less set foot in it. I dined on board ship, disembarked,
And ran into you.

DÉSIRÉE   Some situation! I'm nearly a wreck. What's that ship
You're talking about?

MENAECHMUS II   Oh, an old prewar propeller job,
Wood and canvas, patched in a million places; transportation,
I guess, runs on force of habit. She's got so many pegs
Pounded in now, one right up against the next, she looks like
the rack
You see in a fur-seller's store where the strips are hung all in a
row.

DÉSIRÉE Oh, do stop now, please, making fun, and come on in
with me.

MENAECHMUS II My dear woman, you're looking for some other
man, not me.

DÉSIRÉE I don't know you, Menaechmus? the son of Moschus,
Born at Syracuse in Sicily, when Agathocles ruled,
And after him, Phintia; then Leporello passed on the power
After his death to Hiero, so that Hiero is now the man in con-
trol?

MENAECHMUS II Well, that information seems certainly accurate,
Miss.

MESSENIO   By God Himself! Is the woman *from* Syracuse to have
This all down so pat?

MENAECHMUS II   By the various gods, I don't see
How I can now really decline that offer she's making.

MESSENIO   Please do, I mean *don't* step over that doorstep!
You're gone if you do.

MENAECHMUS II   Pipe down. This is working out well.
I'll admit to anything she says, if I can just take advantage
Of the good time in store. Mademoiselle, a moment ago
I was holding back on purpose, afraid that my wife might hear
About the silk dress and our dinner date. I'm all set
Now, anytime you are.

DÉSIRÉE   You won't wait for Soft Hair?

MENAECHMUS II   No, let's brush *him* off; I don't care a whisker
if he never, . . .
And besides, when he does, I don't want him let in

DÉSIRÉE   Heavens to Castor!
I'm more than happy to comply with that one. But now,
Just one thing, darling, you know what I'd like you to do?

MENAECHMUS II   All you need do is name it.

DÉSIRÉE   That sweet silk dress: send it over
To the Persian's place, the embroiderer's shop. I want
It taken in, and a pattern I've specially designed added to it.

MENAECHMUS II   What a good idea! It won't look at all like the
dress
I stole, if my wife should happen to meet you in town.

DÉSIRÉE   Good. Take it with you, then, when you go.

MENAECHMUS II   Yes, of course.

DÉSIRÉE   And now let's go on in.

MENAECHMUS II   Right away. I've just got to speak
To him for a minute. Hey, Messenio, hop over here!

MESSENIO   What's cooking?

MENAECHMUS II   Jump, boy.

MESSENIO   What's all the hurry?

MENAECHMUS II   We're all the hurry, that's what. I know what
you'll say.

MESSENIO   You're a dope.

MENAECHMUS II   Nope, I'm a fiend. I've already stolen
some loot.

Real loot. This is a big deal: Operation Mix-up.
And I'm one up already without even throwing up earthworks.
Race off, fast as you can, and drape all those sea troops [*points
to the sailors*]
In the local bar, on the double. Stay where you are then,
Until just before sunset, when it's time to come pick me up.

MESSENIO Really, Commander, you're not *on* to those call girls.

MENAECHMUS II You manage your affairs, I'll handle mine, and
you
Can hang up and stay there. If I get into trouble, it's me
Who'll suffer for it, not you. That girl isn't crazy, she's dumb
And doesn't know what's up, at least as far as I can see,
Or where could this high-priced, pretty little dress have come
from? [*Exit.*]

MESSENIO I give up. You've gone, have you? In there? You're
gone,
And done for. The pirate ship's got the rowboat on the run,
And you'll end up in the drink, *Menaechmus on the rocks.*
But who am I, a dumb slave, to try to outfox
That woman, with my hopes of showing Menaechmus the ropes?
He bought me to listen to him: I'm not in command.
Come on, kids, let's do what he says. But I'll be on hand
Later on, as he wanted, and drag him out to dry land.

ACT THREE

Scene One

[PENICULUS]

PENICULUS   In all my born days—and it's more than thirty years'
   worth—I've never
Pulled a boner like this, I'm a treacherous fiend, and this time
I guess I've really transgressed. Imagine my missing a meal!
And why? I got involved in listening to a public speech
And while I stood around gawking, all open mouth and ears,
Menaechmus made his getaway and got back to his girl,
And didn't want *me* along, I suppose. May the heavenly gods
Crack down on whoever it was that thought up public speeches,
That invented this out-of-doors way to use up people's good time
Who haven't any. Shouldn't the audience consist only of those
With time on their hands? And shouldn't they perhaps be fined
If they fail to attend those meetings where someone gets up
In public and starts sounding off? There are people enough
With nothing much to do, who eat only one meal a day,
Never dine out, or have guests in, and it's to them the duty
To show up at meetings or official functions should be assigned.
If I hadn't stuck around today to listen, I wouldn't
Have lost out on the dinner Menaechmus invited
Me to come to—and I do think he meant it, as sure as I can see
I'm alive. I'll show up, anyway, on the off-chance
There's still something left; the mere hope makes my mouth
   water.
What's this I see? Menaechmus *leaving*, well looped?
That means *dinner's over:* by God, my timing is perfect.
I'll hide over here and watch a bit to see what he does
Before I go up to my host and give him a buzz.

Scene Two

[MENAECHMUS II *and* PENICULUS]

MENAECHMUS II   Calm down in there, woman! I'll bring the dress
   back soon enough,
Expertly, so charmingly changed you won't even know it.

PENICULUS   Dinner's done, the wine's all gone, the parasite's lost,

27

And *he's* off to the couturi*er*, with that dress in tow.
Is *that* so? I'm not who I am if I take this last bit
In my stride, lying down. Watch how I handle that garment
worker.

MENAECHMUS II   I thank you, immortal gods, each and all of you.
On whom have you ever showered so many good gifts
As you have on me today? And who could have hoped for them
less?
I've dined, I've win*e*d, I've reclined, and at very close quarters,
With one of the most delicious daughters . . . well, I've had it in
the best sense
Of that past tense. And here I am at present, still gifted
With a precious piece of silk. No one else will inherit
These convertible goods, much less wear it. How high am I, its
Heir—O!

PENICULUS   Hell, I can't hear from over here—did he say "hair,"
though?
That's my cue to brush in, isn't it, and sweep up my share?
Hair today and bald tomorrow . . . Drink to me only with
mayonnaise . . .
I'll demand re-dressing . . . I'll scrape something out of this
mess yet.

MENAECHMUS II   She said I stole it from my wife and gave it to
her.
When I realized how wrong she was, of course I began
To agree with everything she said, as if we agreed
On whatever it was we were doing. Need I say more?
I never had so good a time for so little money.

PENICULUS   Here I go; I'm raring to get in my licks.

MENAECHMUS II   Well, well, who's this comes to see me?

PENICULUS   What's that you say,
You featherhead, you worst of all possible, good-for-nothing . . .
man?
Man? You're not even a mistake, you're a premeditated crime,
That's what you are, you shifty little good-for-nothing . . . I just
said that . . .
So-and-so. And so you spirited yourself away
From me at the forum a while ago, and celebrated my funeral
At this cheerful dinner your friend just couldn't attend?
Some nerve, when you said I was invited to share it with you.

MENAECHMUS II   Look, kiddo, what's with it, with you and me,
that can make
You curse out a man you don't even know? Would you like

A nice hole in the head in return for turning loose your lip?

PENICULUS   God damn it to God damn. That hole's already in my
stomach,
You gave my mouth the slip.

MENAECHMUS II   What's your name, kid,
Anyway? Spit that much out.

PENICULUS   Still being funny,
As if you didn't know?

MENAECHMUS II   As far as I know, no.
God knows I never saw you before today, never knew you,
Whoever you are. I do know, though, if you don't
Get funny with me I won't make it hard for you.

PENICULUS   For heck's sake, Menaechmus, wake up!

MENAECHMUS II   For Hercules' sake,
I'm up and walking around. I'm completely convinced of it.

PENICULUS   But you don't recognize me?

MENAECHMUS II   If I did, I wouldn't say I didn't.

PENICULUS   You don't know your old parasite pal?

MENAECHMUS II   It's your old paralyzed dome
That's slipped, or cracked. You'd better have it patched up and
fixed.

PENICULUS   All right. Here's a question for you. Did you, or did
you not,
Sneak a dress out from under your own wife's nose today,
And give it to dear Désirée?

MENAECHMUS II   For Hercle's sake, no.
I don't happen to be married, and I didn't happen to
Give it to Désirée, and I didn't happen to fasten onto
A dress. Are you quite sure you've got it in the head, enough?

PENICULUS   Well, that's that, I guess. *Caput! E pluribus* be none.
Of course I didn't meet you coming out of your house and wear-
ing
The dress, just a while ago?

MENAECHMUS II   Ohhhhh for *sex'* sake! [*very effemi-
nate sibilants*]
You think we're all fairy fine fellows just because you're such
A *native* dancer, in a perfect fright at what's under our tights?
You say I put on a dress, and I wore it?

PENICULUS   Could of swore it, on Hercules' head.

MENAECHMUS II   Don't bring him up,
He was a he-man, but you aren't even a me-man:
You don't even know who you are or I am, you absolute nut.
You'd better take the cure; you're asking for trouble from the
gods.

PENICULUS   Yeee gods, that's it! Now nobody's going to stop me
from going
Straight to your wife to spill the beans about you and your
schemes.
You've creamed me, and I'm whipped. But banquet boy, just
you wait
Until this stuff starts coming back at you. That dinner you ate
And I never got to, is going to give you bad dreams.

MENAECHMUS II   What's going on around here? Is everyone I see
Planted here on purpose to make fun of me? And what for?
And here comes another, whoever it is, out that door.

Scene Three

[MENAECHMUS II *and* MAID]

MAID   Menaechmus, Désirée would like you to take
This bracelet to the jeweler's, as long as you're going downtown
With the dress, and have this piece of gold worked into it.

MENAECHMUS II   Oh, glad to take care of both things, of course,
and anything
Else you want done along those lines; you only need mention it.

MAID   You remember the bracelet, don't you?

MENAECHMUS II   It's just a gold bracelet.

MAID   But this is the one you sneaked out of your wife's jewel box
And stole from her.

MENAECHMUS II   I don't do things like that, I'm damned sure.

MAID   Well, if you don't recognize it . . . look, you'd better give it
back to me.

MENAECHMUS II   Hold on . . . I think I do remember it now. . . .
Yes, that's the one I gave her, that's it all right.
But where are the armlets I gave Désirée when I gave her
The bracelet?

MAID   You never gave her no armlets at all.

MENAECHMUS II   Oh yes, that's right, it was just the bracelet,
come to think of it.

MAID   Can I tell her you'll have this fixed up?

MENAECHMUS II   Yes, I'll take care of it.

MAID   And look, be a dear, and have him design me some earrings,
Won't you, teardrop style, six dollars of gold work in each?
If you do, you'll be *persona* terribly *grata* to me, your
Obedient, co-operative servant, the next time you visit.

MENAECHMUS II   Why of course. Just give me the gold, and I'll
stand the cost
Of having it set.

MAID   Oh, you furnish the gold, why don't you?
And I'll pay you back later.

MENAECHMUS II   No, no, after you, my fair lady.
You let me pay you back later, and I'll pay twice as much.

MAID   I don't have the gold at the moment.

MENAECHMUS II   When you get it, I'll take it.

MAID   Is there anything else, kind sir?

MENAECHMUS II   No, just say I'll handle this.

[*Exit* MAID.]

And make a quick turnover on the market value of the stuff.
She's gone in? Yes, I see she's closed the door.
The gods must be on my side the way they're helping me out,
Enriching me, and doing me favors. But why hang around
When now is my chance to get away and out of reach
Of these foxy, and I must say, sexy, confidence women?
Come on, Menaechmus, my boy, my own likeness, enjoy
Your rapture; and pick up your feet, old chap, let those sandals
   slap.
Here goes the laurel lei for today [*throws it right*], but I think
   I'll go this way,
In case they come looking for me; they can follow this lead
In the wrong direction. I'll dash off and make enough speed
To head off my slave, I hope, and tell that good lad
The good news about the goods we've acquired. Won't he be
   glad?

ACT FOUR

Scene One

[WIFE OF MENAECHMUS *and* PENICULUS]

WIFE   I suppose I'm supposed to submit to total frustration
Because I married a man who steals everything in the house
He can lay hands on and carts it off to his mistress?

PENICULUS   Not so loud, please. You'll catch him with the goods,
   I promise.
Come over here. Now look over there. He was taking
Your dress to the coutur*er*; he was well looped and weaving
Downtown with the same dress he snuck from your closet today.
And look, there's the laurel loop he had on, lying on the ground.
Now do you believe me? He must have gone in that direction,
If you'd like to follow up his tracks. Hey, we're in luck:
Here he comes back, just this moment; but not with the dress.

WIFE   What should I do?

PENICULUS   Oh, what you always do, start nagging,
Nag him to pieces; don't take it, let him have it, I say.
Meanwhile, let's duck over here on the sly and not let him
See us. He'll tangle himself in the birdcatchers' net.

Scene Two

[WIFE, PENICULUS, *and* MENAECHMUS I]

MENAECHMUS I   This is some social system we've got going
   here,
The troublesome custom of patrons and clients:
Bothersome clients, and jittery patrons, who fear
They may not have a big enough following. Compliance
And conformity to habit require even the best of us
To just make the most of it; and as for the rest of those
Trapped in place in the status race, let's face it,
They're coming at us, pushing forward from the ends
To swell out the middle. And it isn't *fides,* it's *res*
That matters in the clientele deal, which depends,
Not on the client's value as man and as friend,
But simply on his assets. Money is what he's worth
And you must amass it to show off less dearth

32

Of a deficit than the next aristocrat. You give a wide berth
To the poor man who needs you, however fine he may seem,
But if some rich bastard shows up and wants you to use
Your influence, you're ready to go to any extreme
To hang onto him. That's the scheme, and does it confuse
Us poor patrons with a gang of fast-breaking scofflaws
To stand up for in court? Thereby hang the loss
And the profits for us poor patricians. The clients' position
Is: pressure on the middle. He's got the money,
We've got the rank, we need his dough and he needs our thanks.
It's only lucky the prolies don't rate either of any;
Thanks heavens, they're not powerful, just many.
    I'm from a good family and entitled to go into court
And represent as I wish some client who's short
Of the necessary social credentials. And, confidentially,
I say a lot that I wish I didn't have to. A lawyer can manage
To do this pretty well if he concentrates on it; and damages
Are his principal concern: to collect for, to sue for, to affirm
What is said to be false, and deny what is said to be true for.
On behalf of some client whose character makes him squirm
He will bribe the witnesses or rehearse them in what to do.
When the client's case comes up on the calendar, of course
That's a day we have to be on hand too, and be resourceful
In speaking up professionally in defense of his actions, awful
And impossible to defend though they are.
It's either a private hearing at the bar;
Or a public proceeding before a jury with people in the con-
    gregation;
Or a third form it takes is what you would call arbitration,
When a mediator is appointed to decide this special situation.
    Well, today a client of mine had me right on the ropes;
His case came up as a private hearing, and my hopes
Of doing what I'd planned to today, and doing
It with the person I wanted to, have drooped and dropped near
    to ruin;
He kept me and kept me; there was angle after angle.
He was obviously at fault, with his wrong, tangled
Illegal action, and I knew it when I went in.
So in arguing the case I laid it on pretty thin,
And pleaded *extenuating circumstances;* that's a logical maze
And a judge's jungle, but a lawyer's paradise.
I summed up the case in the most complicated terms
I could summon up, overstating, sliding words like worms
Off the track, leaving a lot out when the need
Of the argument indicated, and the magistrate agreed
To drop the proceedings; he granted permission
For a settlement by *sponsio.*

There's a legal ounce for you, of the words we pronounce in due
    process,
Full of awful, responsible-sounding phrases like: I promise
You this *sponsio* I owe you, et cetera. What it comes down to
Is that a civil hearing can be brought to an end by payment
Of a fixed fee known as a forfeit or *sponsio,* a defrayment
Of the expenses plus a sum added on: call it "costs
And considerations" if you will, in consideration for the lost
Time and money involved. What happened today was that I
Had worked hard and fast to convince the judge that my
Client should be allowed to settle for costs and considerations.
The judge came around; and I was set to leave for the celebration
Of a good time at Désirée's party, when what did my other
    smarty party
Of a client pull but an "Oh, well . . . I don't know about that
sponsio . . .
I don't think I ought to flounce in with a lot of money all at once
You know . . . I'm not so sure I've even got it. Are you sure
That's the way we want it to go, the case, et cetera?" The totally
    pure
Imbecile, caught redhanded, absolutely without a legal leg to
    stand on
And three unimpeacheable witnesses were waiting just to get
    their hands on
Him and wring his neck! He nearly let it come up for trial.
And that's where I've been all this while.
    May the gods, all the gods, blast that fool
Who wrecked my beautiful day
And they might as well, while they're at it, lay
Into me for thinking I could steal
Off to town and look the forum over that way
Without being spotted and tapped for something dutiful.
No doubt, I've messed up a day
That promised to be quite alluring
From the moment I told Désirée
To set things up nicely for dinner. All during
The time I've been detained, she's been waiting for me
And here I am at last, the first instant I could break free.
If she's angry, I suppose she has some reason to be.
But perhaps the dress I purloined from my wife won't annoy her
In the least, and I'll win this one too, as my own lawyer.

PENICULUS   What do you say to that?

WIFE   That I've made a bad marriage
With an unworthy husband.

PENICULUS   Can you hear well enough where you are?

WIFE   All too well.

MENAECHMUS I   The smart thing for me is to go on in there
Where I can count on a pretty good time.

PENICULUS   Just you wait,
Bad times are just around the corner.

WIFE [*confronting him*]   You think you got away
With it, do you? This time you'll pay up, with interest.

PENICULUS   That's it, let him have it.

WIFE   Pulled a fast one on the sly, didn't you?

MENAECHMUS I   What fast one are you referring to, dear?

WIFE   You're asking me?

MENAECHMUS I   Should I ask him, instead?

WIFE   Take your paws off me.

PENICULUS   That's the way!

MENAECHMUS I   Why so cross?

WIFE   You ought to know.

PENICULUS   He knows, all right, he's just faking.

MENAECHMUS I   With reference to what?

WIFE   To that dress, that's what.

MENAECHMUS I   That dress that's what what?

WIFE   A certain silk dress.

PENICULUS   Why is your face turning pale?

MENAECHMUS I   It isn't.

PENICULUS   Not much paler than a thin silk dress, it isn't.
And don't think you can go off and eat dinner behind my back.
Keep pitching into him.

MENAECHMUS I   Won't you hang up for a moment?

PENICULUS   God damn it, no, I won't. He's shaking his head
To warn me not to say anything.

MENAECHMUS I   God damn it, yourself,
If I'm shaking my head, or winking or blinking or nodding.

PENICULUS   Cool! Shakes his head to deny he was shaking his
head.

MENAECHMUS I   I swear to you, wife, by Jupiter, and all the other
gods—
I hope that's reinforced strong enough to satisfy you—
I did *not* nod at that nut.

PENICULUS   Oh, she'll accept that
On good faith. Now let's return to the first case.

MENAECHMUS I   What first case?

PENICULUS   The case of the costly couturier's place.
The dress-fixer's.

MENAECHMUS I   Dress? What dress?

PENICULUS   Perhaps I'd better bow out.
After all, it's my client who's suing for redress of grievance
And now she can't seem to remember a thing she wanted to ask
you.

WIFE   Oh dear, I'm just a poor woman in trouble.

MENAECHMUS I   Come on, tell me,
What is it? One of the servant's upset you by answering back?
You can tell me about it; I'll see that he's punished.

WIFE   Don't be silly.

MENAECHMUS I   Really, you're *so* cross. I don't like you that way.

WIFE   Don't be silly.

MENAECHMUS I   Obviously, it's one of the servants you're mad at?

WIFE   Don't be silly.

MENAECHMUS I   You're not mad at me, are you?

WIFE   Now you're not being so silly.

MENAECHMUS I   But, for God's sake, I haven't done anything.

WIFE   Don't start being silly
All over again.

MENAECHMUS I   Come on, dear, what is it that's wrong
And upsets you so?

PENICULUS   Smooth husband, smooths everything over.

MENAECHMUS I   Oh, hang up, I didn't call you.

WIFE   *Please* take your paw off me.

PENICULUS   That's the way, lady, stick up for your rights. We'll
teach him
To run off to dinner and not wait for me, and then stagger out
Afterwards and lurch around in front of the house still wearing
His wreath and having a good laugh on me.

MENAECHMUS I   Dear God in heaven,
If I've even eaten yet, much less gone into that house.

PENICULUS   You don't say?

MENAECHMUS I   That's right, I don't say, you're damned right I
don't.

PENICULUS   God, that's some nerve. Didn't I see you over there
just now,

In front of the house, standing there with a wreath on your head?
Didn't I hear you telling me I was way off my nut, and insisting
You didn't know who I was, and were a stranger here yourself?

MENAECHMUS I   But I left you some time ago, and I'm just getting
back.

PENICULUS   That's what you say. You didn't think I'd fight back,
did you?
Well, by God, I've spilled the whole thing to your wife.

MENAECHMUS I   Saying what?

PENICULUS   How should I know? Ask her.

MENAECHMUS I   How about it, dear?
What all has this type told you? Come on, don't repress it;
Won't you tell me what it is?

WIFE   As if you didn't know,
You ask me.

MENAECHMUS I   If I knew, for God's sake, I wouldn't be asking.

PENICULUS   This is really some man the way he fakes out. Look,
you can't
Keep it from her, she knows all about it. By God in wherever he
is,
I practically dictated it.

MENAECHMUS I   Dictated what?

WIFE   All right. Since you seem not to have an ounce of shame
left,
And you won't own up, give me your undivided attention.
This is why I'm upset and this is what he told me. I repeat,
I'm not really "cross"; I'm double-crossed, and doubly upset.
Someone sneaked one of my very best dresses right out of my
house.

MENAECHMUS I   A dress? Right out of my house?

PENICULUS   *Listen* to that louse,
Trying to scratch his way into your affections. Look, Menaech-
mus,
We're not playing matched towels in the doctor's bathroom
Marked "Hisia" and "Hernia"; we're discussing a valuable dress,
And its *hers* not yours, and she's lost it, at least for the time
being.
If *yours* were missing it would really be missing for good.

MENAECHMUS I   Will you please disappear? Now dear, what's your
point of view?

WIFE   The way I see it, one of my best silk dresses is not at home.

MENAECHMUS I   I wonder who might have taken it.

WIFE   I'm pretty sure
I know a man who knows who took it, because he did.

MENAECHMUS I   Who dat?

WIFE   Welllll . . . I'd like us to think of a certain Menaechmus.

MENAECHMUS I   Some man, just like us! Isn't that the fancy one,
   that man?
   But he's a mean man. And who the hell are all the men you
   mean
   Named Menaechmus?

WIFE   You, that's what I say, you.

MENAECHMUS I   Who accuses me to you?

WIFE   I do, for one.

PENICULUS   I do too. And I say you gave it to a dear little Daisy.

MENAECHMUS I   I? Me? I'm that mean aechmus who . . .

WIFE   Yes, you, that's who,
   You brute, et tu.

PENICULUS   You who too too too . . .
   What is this, the Owl Movement from the Bird Symphony?
   My ears are feeling the strain of that to-who refrain.

MENAECHMUS I   I swear, wife, by Jupiter, and all other gods within
   hearing distance—
   And I hope that's a strongly enough reinforced religious insistence—
   That I did not give . . .

PENICULUS   But we can appeal to Hercules and he's
   Even stronger, that we're not exactly not telling the truth.

MENAECHMUS I   That technically I did not give it, I only conveyed
   it
   To Daisy today; you see, she doesn't have it, she's just using it.

WIFE   I don't go around lending out your jacket or cloak.
   A woman ought to lend out women's clothes, a man men's.
   You'll bring back the dress?

MENAECHMUS I   I'll see that that's done.

WIFE   If you know what's good for you, you will, I'm here to
   assure you.
   You won't get back in this house unless you're carrying that
   dress.
   I'm going in.

PENICULUS   What about me and my work?

WIFE   I'll pay you back when something is stolen from your house.

PENICULUS   Oh God, that means never. There's nothing in my
place worth stealing.
Well, Husband and Wife, may the gods do their very worst for
you both!
I'll run along now, to the forum. It's quite plain to see
I've lost out, and lost my touch, with this family.
[*Exit; never returns.*]

MENAECHMUS I   My wife thinks she's making life hard for me,
shutting me out
Of the house. As if I didn't have a much more pleasant place
To go into. Fallen from your favor, have I? I imagine
I'll bear up under that and prove pleasing to an even more
desirable
Favorite. Désirée won't lock me out, she'll lock me in.
I guess I'll go in there and ask her to *lend* back the dress
I *conveyed* to her this morning, and buy her something much
better.
Hey, where's the doorman? Open up, somebody, and tell
Désirée to come out; there's someone to see her.

Scene Three

[DÉSIRÉE *and* MENAECHMUS I]

DÉSIRÉE   Who's calling me?

MENAECHMUS I   A man who'd be his own enemy
Before he'd be yours.

DÉSIRÉE   Menaechmus, *dahling,* come in!
Why stand out there?

MENAECHMUS I   I bet you can't guess why I'm here.

DÉSIRÉE   Oh, yes I can. You want something sweet from your
honey,
And what's more you'll get it, you naughty little tumblebee.

MENAECHMUS I   As a matter of fact, or thanks heavens, or some-
thing . . .
What I have to have is that silly dress back I gave you
This morning. My wife's found out all about it.
But I'll buy you one worth twice as much, whatever kind you
want,
So be a good girl and romp in there and get it, won't you?

DÉSIRÉE   But I just handed it over to you to take to the Persian's,

Just a while ago, and gave you that bracelet to take to the jeweler
And have the gold added to it.

MENAECHMUS I   The dress and a bracelet?
I think you may find you did no such thing. I gave
The dress to you and then went to the forum, and here
I am looking at you for the first time again since I left you.

DÉSIRÉE Don't look at me, I'll look at you. I see
Just what you're up to, and what I'm down to, for that matter.
You take the stuff off my two trusting hands and then
Do me out of it and pocket the cash for yourself.

MENAECHMUS I I'm not asking for it to cheat you out of it, I
    swear.
I tell you, my wife's cracked the case.

DÉSIRÉE   Well, I didn't ask
For it in the first place. You brought it of your own free will,
And you gave it to me as a gift, you didn't *convey* it, you shyster.
Now you want it back. I give up. You can have the stuff;
Take it away, wear it yourself if you want,
Or let your wife wear it, or lock the loot in your safe.
You're not setting foot in my house from this moment on,
Don't kid yourself about that. I deserve better treatment
From you than being jerked around and laughed at like a clown.
I've been your friend, lover boy—but that's at an end.
From now on, it's strictly for cash, if and when.
Find some other doll to play with and then let her down.

MENAECHMUS I God damn it, don't get so God damn mad. Hey,
    don't go
Off like that, wait a minute! Come back here. You won't?
Oh come on, Dee. Not even for me? You won't? So I see.
She's gone in and locked the door too. And I guess that makes me
Just about the most locked-out fellow in this town today,
Most unwanted man, most unlikely to get in, much less to say
Anything that a wife, or a mistress, might take to be true.
I'll go ask my friends what they think I ought to do.

ACT FIVE

Scene One

[MENAECHMUS II *and* WIFE OF MENAECHMUS I]

MENAECHMUS II It was really pretty dumb of me to put that
  purseful of money
In Messenio's hands, the way I did. He's probably holed up
In some dive, drinking it down, and looking them over.

WIFE I think I'll just take a look and see how soon husband
  Wends his way home. There he is now. And all's well for me:
  He's got the dress with him.

MENAECHMUS II   Where in hell has Messenio wandered off to?

WIFE I'll go up and welcome him now in the terms he deserves.
  Aren't you ashamed to show up in my sight, you mistake
  Of a man . . . I mean, you deliberate premeditated crime,
  Tricked out with that fancy gown?

MENAECHMUS II   I don't get it, do I?
  What's on your mind, my good woman?

WIFE   How dare you address me?
  How dare you utter a single slimy syllable, you snake?

MENAECHMUS II What have I done that's so bad I don't dare
  address you?

WIFE You must have cast-iron nerves to inquire about that.

MENAECHMUS II I don't know if you read much, lady, but
  Hecuba:
The Greeks always called her a bitch. I suppose you know why?

WIFE As a matter of fact, no. I don't.

MENAECHMUS II   Because she acted the way
  You're acting right now. She kept dumping insults and curses
  On everyone she met, and snarling at, pitching into everyone
  Her eyes lighted on. No wonder they called her a prime bitch.

WIFE I really can't take this kind of abuse any longer.
  I'd much rather never have been married, than submit to
  The kind of dirt you shovel on me the way you do now.

MENAECHMUS II What's it to me whether you like being married
  or not,
Or want to leave your husband? Do all the people around here

41

Tell their stories to every new man that blows into town?

WIFE What stories? I simply won't take it any longer, I tell you.
I'd rather live all alone than put up with you.

MENAECHMUS II For God's sake, then, live alone, as far as I care,
Or as long as Jupiter may decide to grant you the option.

WIFE A few moments ago you were insisting you hadn't sneaked
off
That mantilla-dress of mine, but now you're waving it
In front of my eyes. Aren't you a tiny bit conscience-stricken?

MENAECHMUS II God only knows what kind of a squeeze play
you're pulling,
You whack, you brazen. . . . How dare you say I took this,
When another woman gave it to me to take and have altered?

WIFE By God (my God, this time), a statement like that
Makes me want to . . . and I'm going to send for my father,
And tell him every single horrible thing you've done,
That's what I'll do. Hey, Decio, in there, come out,
And go find my father and ask him to come here with you.
Tell him please to come quickly, I simply have to see him.
I'll show him every single horrible thing you've done to me.

MENAECHMUS II Are you feeling all right? What single horrible
thing?

WIFE You housebreaker-into! You steal my dress and my jewels
From my house and rob your wife of her goods to throw at
The feet of or load in the arms of your girlfriend as loot.
Have I rehearsed the story accurately enough for your ears to
take in?

MENAECHMUS II Lady, you ought to watch your prepositions;
and while you're at it
Could you mix me a sedative of half hemlock, half lime juice?
You must have some hemlock around here. I must be kept *quiet*
If I'm meant to sustain your attacks. I'm not sure I know
Exactly who you think I am. I may have known you
Long ago in the days of Hercules' father-in-law's father.

WIFE Laugh at me all you want, but your father-in-law
Won't stand for that. Here he comes now. Take a good look,
Won't you? Recognize somebody?

MENAECHMUS II   Oh, him? I may have known him . . .
Yes, I did . . . oh sure, I remember old George from the Trojan
War:
He was our Chaplain, bless his old heart. No. I guess not.

I've never seen him before, just as I've never seen
You before either, either of you, before today.

WIFE You say, you don't know me, and you don't know my
father?

MENAECHMUS II You're right. And actually, if you produced your
grandfather,
I'd say the same.

WIFE   One joke after another. What a bother!

Scene Two

[OLD MAN, WIFE and MENAECHMUS II]

OLD MAN Here I come, pushing one foot after the other,
As fast and as far as my age allows, and to meet
This crisis at my own pace, pushing these pedals, progressing
As best I can. Papa isn't planning to pretend,
Though, to anybody, that it's easy. He's not so spry any more.
I'm pretty darned pregnant with years, that's a fact; planted
With a crop of them, if you conceive of me carrying the burden
Of this body. And there's precious little power left. Oh, it's a bad
deal,
This business of being old. We're stuck with the bulk
Of our unwanted goods. Maybe we get more than we bargained
for
Out of life. Old age brings the most of the worst when it comes,
To the ones who want it the least. If I named every pain
It bestows on us oldsters, I'd be drawing up a long long list,
And you'd have too much to listen to.
                                    I wonder why my daughter
Sent for me all of a sudden? It weighs on my mind
And tugs at my heart to know what's afoot that can bring me
Running over here to see her. She didn't say why she sent for me,
Or tell me what's up. I can figure it out pretty well,
Of course. A quarrel with her husband has sprung up, I bet.
That's the way wives behave who bring a big dowry,
Coming loaded into the marriage and expecting their husbands
To love, honor, and slave away for them. They can be rough.
Of course, the husbands are at fault themselves, every now and
then.
But there's a point at which it's no longer dignified
For the husband to take it any longer. That dear daughter of
mine,

Darn her, never sends for me unless they've both of them been
  doing
Something wrong and a quarrel has started or is definitely
  brewing.
Whatever it is, I'll find out. *Yup!* I'll get brought up on the news.
Here she is now in front of the house. I see how aroused
They both are. She must have lashed into him; he looks
Pretty dashed. *Yup!* Just as I thought. I'll go call to her.

WIFE   I'll go greet father. Good afternoon, Dad. How are you?

OLD MAN   Fine, thank you dear, and you? I hope everything's all
  right.
You didn't send for me because you're in trouble? But you look
Pretty peaked. And why's he standing over there looking mad?
You both look as if you've been trading punches, exchanged a
  few blows
Just for size, to see how it goes. Fill me in on the facts.
Tell me who's to blame, and explain the whole situation.
But briefly, I implore you. Let's not have even one oration,
Much less two.

WIFE   I didn't do anything, Father,
Don't worry. But I can't live here any longer, I can't
Stick it out. Please take me back.

OLD MAN   How did this happen?

WIFE   I've become someone just to be laughed at.

OLD MAN   By whom?

WIFE   By him,
The man, the husband you conferred me on.

OLD MAN   A fight, eh?
That's it, eh? How many times have I told you both of you
To watch out you don't come whining to me with your troubles?

WIFE   How could I watch out, Father dear?

OLD MAN   You really ask that?

WIFE   Only if you don't mind my asking.

OLD MAN   How often have I told you
To put up with your husband? Don't watch where he goes;
Don't see what he does; don't pry into what he's engaged in.

WIFE   But he's crazy about this daisy of a flower girl; and she
  lives right next door.

OLD MAN   That's perfectly natural, and in view of the way you're
  so busy

Keeping an eye on his business, he'll get even dizzier about Daisy,
I just bet you.

WIFE   But he goes over there for drinks all the time.

OLD MAN What's it to you whether he drinks over there? If he
   drinks,
He'll have to do it somewhere. And what's so terrible about that?
You might as well ask him to stop having dinner in town,
Or never bring anyone home for a meal. Are husbands
Supposed to take orders from you? Let them run the house then,
And order the maids around, hand out wool to be carded
And get on with their spinning and weaving.

WIFE   But Father, I ask you
To represent *me,* not to be *his* lawyer in this case.
You're standing here on my side, but you're taking his.

OLD MAN Of course, if he's misbehaved, I'll get after him as much
As I've lit into you, in fact more so. But he seems to be taking
Pretty good care of you, giving you jewels, clothes,
Your servants, furnishing the food. You ought to take a practical,
More sensible view of the thing.

WIFE   But he's rooked me by stealing
Jewels and dresses from my closet at home to sneak off with,
My clothes, my jewels, to dress up that girl he calls on on the
   sly with.

OLD MAN That's some prep . . . I mean proposition, I mean some
   imposition.
I mean, that's terrible if that's going on—if it isn't
Your supposition's as bad, putting an innocent man under sus-
   picion.

WIFE But Dad, he's got them there with him, the dress and that
   sweet
Gold flexible bracelet. He took them to her
And now, since I've found out about it, he's bringing them back.

OLD MAN Well, now, we'll see about that. I'm going to find out
About that. I'm going right over there and ask him, I am.
Oh say, Menaechmus, would you mind telling me, if you don't
Mind, about the matter you've been . . . discussing with her?
I'm curious to know. And why are you looking so down
In the mouth, old fellow? Why's my girl standing over there
By herself, all alone, and so cross?

MENAECHMUS II   I summon all the gods,
And Jupiter Himself Supreme, as they are my witnesses. . . .
Old boy, whoever you are, whatever your name
May happen to be.

OLD MAN   As they are your witnesses to what?
Why do you need such a cloud of high-ranking witnesses?

MENAECHMUS II   That I have not done anything wrong to this
    woman
Who claims that I surreptitiously deprived her
Of this dress and carried it off under suspicious circumstances.

WIFE Well, that's a clear enough lie. He's perjured himself for
    sure.

MENAECHMUS II   If I have ever even set foot inside her house
May I be of all men the most terribly tremendously miserably.

OLD MAN   That's not a very bright thing to wish for, is it? You
    don't say
You've never set foot in the house there you live in, do you,
You stupid goop?

MENAECHMUS II   What's that you're saying about me
Living in that house, you goofy duffer? *I* live *there?*

OLD MAN   You deny it?

MENAECHMUS II   Oh for Hercle's sake, of course I deny it.

OLD MAN   Oh for Hercle's sake right back, you lie if you do
Say you don't, I mean deny it. Unless you moved out last night.
Come here, Daughter, listen: You two haven't moved
Recently, have you?

WIFE   Heavens! Where to? Or why should we have?

OLD MAN   Well, of course, I couldn't know about that.

WIFE   Don't you *get* it?
He's joking around with you.

OLD MAN   All right, Menaechmus, I've taken
Enough of your joking now. Come on, boy, let's get down to
    business.

MENAECHMUS II   *Je vous en prie!* What the hell business have you
    got with me?
In the first place, who the hell are you? And in the second place
I don't owe you any money. Nor her, in the third place.
Who's giving me all this trouble, in the next few places?

WIFE Look, do you notice how his eyes seem to be going all green
All of a sudden? And there's a green tinge developing on the skin
Around his temples and forehead. Look at his eyes glowing red,
Or is it green?

MENAECHMUS II   I wonder if I'd better not pretend I *am* crazy
And scare them away by throwing a fit? They're the ones
Who seem to be insisting on it.

WIFE His arms twitch, his jaw drops.
Oh, Father, what shall I do?

OLD MAN Come here to your father,
My girl, stay as far away as you can from him.

MENAECHMUS II *Ho yo to yo! Tobacco Boy! Take me back to ya!*
I hear ya callin' me out to that happy hunting ground
Deep down in desegregated Damnasia (that's in the Near East),
Callin' your boy to come on out huntin' with his hound dogs!
I hear ya, Bromie Boy, but I jes' cain come near ya.
They won't let me loose from this toothpickin' witch-huntin'
*   northland.*
They's an old foam-covered bitch and she's keeping watch
On my left. And right behind me here they's a goat,
An ole toothpickin' garlic-stinking but I mean old goat,
Who's been buttin' down innocent citizens all of his life
By bringing up things that ain't true against them
And then rounding up people to come listen to them refute
*   them.*

OLD MAN I'm afraid your mind's been affected.

MENAECHMUS II I've just swallowed an oracle
Of Apollo that orders me instantly to start setting about
Finding two red hot searchlights to put her eyes out with.

WIFE Goodness, what a prepositionous preposterous proposition,
Father. He's threatening to burn out my eyes in.

MENAECHMUS II Touché, for me. They say I'm raving, but they
Are rather wild at the moment. The straightjacket's on the other
foot.

OLD MAN Oh, my poor girl.

WIFE Yes, Father?

OLD MAN What shall we do?
Suppose I send for the slaves in a hurry; I'll go
And bring them myself, to take him away and chain him
Safely at home before he starts getting more destructive.

MENAECHMUS II Trapped! Strung up by my own guitar! If I don't
Improvise something soon they'll come on and cart me away.
Yes I hear you, sugar Radiant Apollo! I'll follow through
With my fists (you insist?) and spare not the laying on of hands.
Punch that woman in the jaw, you say, according to your law,
Unless she disappears from my view and gets herself gone
The holy hell and crucified crutch of a cross
Out of my way? Apollo, I'll do what you say!

OLD MAN Scoot into the house, fast as poss, or he'll slug you.

WIFE   Scoot I go,
Father, *ergo,* soon I'll be out of the way. But please, Father,
Keep stalling him, don't let him slip out of reach. Don't you
agree,
I'm a most put-upon specimen of woman to put up with that?

MENAECHMUS II I've got rid of her: not bad. Now for dad. You
slob,
Listen, you baggy bearded, quavering long-since-past father,
You shriveled old, dried-up grasshopper—and besides your voice's
changed,
Singing your Glorias Swansong soprano in your second child-
hood.
What's that, Apollo? Thou sayest I should smashest his frame,
His bones, and the joints that hook them to same? I'm game.
Smashomin, you say, with his owncluboff? Use his cane?

OLD MAN There'll be trouble for you if you lay a finger on me,
Or move any closer.

MENAECHMUS II   *Oh sir, Apollo? The following*
Changes in wording? Take one each two-headed axe
And split right down through the frame, through the guts to the
bones,
And hack his back to bits and make slivers of his liver and his
Whole intestinal tract, don't just cudgel the codger?
Roger to tower. Look at that geezer cower and run for cover.

OLD MAN I suppose I'd better look to my laurels, what's left of
them, withered
As an old man's may be. I'll look after me. He's a menace,
That's clear enough. He just may decide to take it out on my
hide.

MENAECHMUS II For god's sake, Apollo, what's this? Another mes-
sage? The traffic's
Getting heavy. *Take four wild bucking broncos and hitch*
Them up to a buckboard, and climb aboard and drive them over
This lion, this bearded biped, this antique toothless
Gumclicking biped with bad breath? Roger, I'm mounted, oh joy
To Yoy, King Roy Apolloy. I'm holding that wagon's reins
And flicking the whip already. Up there, you double pair
Of quadruplets. Drum it out on the ground when you trample
him down.
Bend your knees, noble steeds, be nimble as the breeze.
Pound you there, pound.

OLD MAN   He's coming at me with two pairs
Of horses?

MENAECHMUS II Whoa there! *Yes, Apollo, of course I hear you*
Telling me to launch my attack against him, yes, him
Over there, and murder him. Whoa there! Who's hauling me back
By the hair, and pulling me out of the chariot? Who does this
Reverses the very command and eeeeeeedict of Apollo.

OLD MAN It's really this poor fellow who's having the attack, I
would say.
And he's really having one, the full scale deluxe one with nuts in
it,
God save us all. Well, that's how it is, by God. Here's a fellow
Completely crackers, and a minute ago he was perfectly rational.
When that mad stuff hits you it lands hard all of a sudden.
I'll go ask the doctor to get here as soon as he can. [*Exit.*]

MENAECHMUS II [*alone, faces audience and addresses them across
the stagefront*] Now I ask you, have those two at last gotten
out of my sight,
Who forced me to play this mad role, when, as *you* know,
I'm perfectly well? This is my chance to pick up and go
Winging back to my ship, don't you think, quick as a wink,
While I'm still safe and sound? Listen, if you're still around
When the old man comes back, you won't tell—he'll be in a
rage—
Where I went when I left the stage? You won't say where I can
be found? [*Exit.*]

Scene Three

[OLD MAN *and* DOCTOR]

OLD MAN My back's stiff with sitting, my eyes nearly worn out
with looking,
Hanging around waiting for God darn that darn medicine man
To finish with his patients and meet this emergency.
Well *finally* he's pulled himself away—not much urgency
Either, from his victims. He's his own worst pain in the neck!
Such a specialist, in name-dropping at least, of who's on his list
Of big shots with big troubles only he can fix. When I insisted
He hike over here, he said "Right away," but first he must set
This broken leg, to the Greater Glory of Aesculapius,
And then put an arm back in place, On Behalf of Apollo.
Which half of Apollo beats the Belvedere out of me: but I see
Him racing over now, weaving down the track like an ant
With lumbago. It's just his ego slows him down, the hot airman.

Putting those pieces together! What is he, a repairman,
A tinker, a joiner at heart? Are his patients all coming apart?

DOCTOR   Now let us see, my man. . . . You described the case of
the diseased
As *larvated, id est,* he sees actual, live, dead ghost spooks?
Or *cerebrated, id est,* perturbated footzled left lobar cavity?
Which is of course only a false hallucination and would show
Some degree of mental inquietude. Would you be so good
As to describe the condition again, so I can decide
What to prescribe or proscribe, indeed just how to proceed?
Did you mention a species of *Hibernating* coma, a kind of
Tendency to feel sleepy all the time? Or did you more plainly see
A subaqueous subcutaneous *slurpation,* like say, water on the
knee?

OLD MAN   The reason I've brought you in on the case is to find
out
From you just what's wrong and ask you to cure it.

DOCTOR   How true,
And I'll do it to perfection, never fear; upon my profession
I assure you he'll be quite well again.

OLD MAN   You'll give him
The most careful attention?

DOCTOR   First-class care, rest assured.
My word, Deluxe! Private room; personal visits from me.
I'll see him daily and ponder him most thoughtfully,
Heave hundreds of luxury sighs. He'll rate a thrill
Being ill; and so will you when you see the bill.

OLD MAN   Shh. Here's our man. Let's watch and see what he does.

Scene Four

[OLD MAN, DOCTOR, *and* MENAECHMUS I]

MENAECHMUS I   By God in heaven, if this hasn't been the worst
Of all possible days for me! Everything's gone blooey.
What I planned to do on the sly, that particular parasite,
Peniculus, brought to light, and flooded me with shame and
remorse
In the process. Some Ulysses type, doping out this dirty deal
For his own best protector and patron. Why that . . . sure as I
live,
I'll do him right out of his ensuing existence, I'll unroll

His scroll for him. *His* existence? I'm a fool
To call *his* what's actually mine. I'm the one who brought him up
By wining and dining him. It was my subsistence he lived on:
All he ever managed was coexistence. I'll snuff out
That half of his light by cutting off the supplies.
As for that mercenary Daisy, all I can say is she
Acted quite in keeping with the character of a kept woman,
And I suppose that's human, if meretricious. A very meretricious
And a happy new year to her. When in doubt, just give money.
All I did was ask her for the dress to return to my wife
And she claimed she'd already handed it over. Turned it over,
I bet, to some dealer for cash. Crash! Oh God in heaven,
Did any man ever let himself in for this big a cave-in?

OLD MAN   You hear that?

DOCTOR   He says he's unhappy.

OLD MAN   Go on up to him.

DOCTER   Meeeeenaechmus, *ciao!* How are you? Why expose your
   arm
That way? Exposure can aggravate your serious condition.

MENAECHMUS I   Why don't you go hang up, yourself, on the near-
   est branch?

OLD MAN   Notice anything peculiar?

DOCTOR   Anything? The whole thing,
That's what I notice. This case couldn't be kept under control
By a mountain of miltowns. Menaechmus, just a word with
   you, please.

MENAECHMUS I   What's up, Doc?

DOCTOR   You are. Answer a few questions, please,
And take them in order. First, what color wine do you drink?
White wine, or red?

MENAECHMUS   Oh, my crucified crotch!
What's that to you?

DOCTOR   I seem to detect a slight tendency
To rave, here.

MENAECHMUS I   Why not color-quiz me on bread?
Do I take purple, cerise, or golden red? As a rule,
Do I eat fish with their feathers or birds with their scales and all?

OLD MAN   I win! Ill, eh? Pu! Can't you hear he's delirious? Hurry
   up
With that sedative, can't you? Why wait for the fit to come on?

DOCTOR Just hold on a bit. I've a few more questions to ask.

OLD MAN You'll finish him off with the questions you keep inventing.

DOCTOR Do your eyes ever feel like they're starting out of your head?

MENAECHMUS I What do you take me for, you seahorse doctor, a lobster?

DOCTOR Do your bowels rumble powerfully, as far as you can tell?

MENAECHMUS I They're perfectly still when I'm full; when hungry, they grumble.

DOCTOR Well now, that's a perfectly straightforward, digestible answer,
Not the word of a nut. You sleep until dawn, and sleep well?

MENAECHMUS I I sleep right through, if I've paid all my bills. Listen, you
Special investigator, I wish to heaven the gods would crack down on you.

DOCTOR Ah, now, to judge from that statement, he's being irrational.

OLD MAN Oh no, that's a wise saying, worthy of Nestor, compared
To what he was saying a while back, when he called his own wife
A stark raving bitch.

MENAECHMUS I   What's that you say I said?

OLD MAN You're out of your head, that's what I say.

MENAECHMUS I   Who's out of what? Me?

OLD MAN Yes, you, that's who. Boo! Threatening to flatten me out
With a four-horsepower chariot. I can swear to it.
I saw you with my own eyes. I charge you with it.

MENAECHMUS I Ah, but here's what I know about you. You purloined the crown
Of Jupiter, his sacred crown, and were locked up in jail.
That's what I know about you. And when they let you out,
It was to put you under the yoke and whip you in public,
With birch rods. That's what I know about you. And then, too,
You killed your own father and sold off your mother as a slave,
That's what I know about you. Don't you think that might possibly do

As a reasonably sound reply to the charges you're letting fly?

OLD MAN Oh hurry up, Doctor, for Hercle's sake, and do what
    you ought to.
Can't you see, the man's *off?*

DOCTOR   You know what I think is best?
Have him brought over to my place.

OLD MAN   You're sure?

DOCTOR   Sure, why not?
I'll be able to treat him there by the very latest methods.

OLD MAN Good. You know best.

DOCTOR   I assure you, Menaechmus, you'll lap up
Super tranquilizers for twenty days.

MENAECHMUS I   Is that medicine
Your madness? I'll gore you, hanging there, for thirty days.

DOCTOR [*aside*] Go call the help, to carry him over to my house.

OLD MAN [*aside*] How many men do we need?

DOCTOR [*aside*]   At least four, to judge
From the way he's raving at present.

OLD MAN [*aside*]   They're practically here.
I'll go run and get them. You stay right here, Doctor, do,
And keep a close eye on him.

DOCTOR [*aside*]   No. As a matter of fact,
I think I'll be off for home, and make the preparations
To receive him. There's quite a lot to do. You go get the help;
Have them bring him to me.

OLD MAN [*aside*]   He's as good as carried there already.

DOCTOR I'm off.

OLD MAN   So am I.

MENAECHMUS I   Now I'm alone. That father-in-law
And that doctor have gone, somewhere or other. But what in
    God's name
Makes these men insist I'm insane? I've never been sick
A day in my life, and I'm not ailing now. I don't start fights,
Or dispute everything that comes up. I wish others well
When I meet them, quite calmly, I recognize people I know,
And speak to them civilly enough. I wonder if they,
Who absurdly declare that I'm mad, since they're in the wrong,
Aren't in fact crazy themselves? I wish I knew what to do.
I'd like to go home, but my wife won't allow it—as for that place
    [*points to* DÉSIRÉE'S *house*]

No one will let me in there, Well, it's all worked out
All right; worked me out of house and home. So I guess
I'll stick around here. I imagine, by the time night comes
I'll be welcome to enter the right one of these two homes.

Scene Five

[MESSENIO]

MESSENIO   God slave the king!
  And of me I sing.
  Or rather, the slave's the thing
  I present and I represent.
  The good slave, intent
  On making his master content,
  Looks after his master's affairs.
  Arranging and planning, he never spares
  Any effort in lavishing cares
  On everything that needs being done.
  When the master's away, he handles all alone
  Problems that keep coming up, and he solves them
  As well as the boss could, himself, all of them;
  And sometimes manages the whole business better than master.
  You need a good sense of balance, to fend off disaster
  From your legs and your back. And you've got to remember
  That your throat and your stomach are not the most vital
      members.
  If you go off guzzling and eating, instead of performing,
  When you come back you're in for a beating and a good body-
      warming.
        May I remind all the shiftless delinquents who keep hanging
        back
  From doing their work, of the price all masters exact
  From good-for-nothings, men they can't count on, in fact?
        Lashes, and chains;
        Turning those wheels at the mill
        Until you begin to feel
        Your brains churning loose and writhing like eels.
        You'll be starved and left out to sleep in the cold open
        fields.
        That's the wages of laziness.
        Not to fear earning that would be the worst sort of craziness.
  Therefore, I've decided, for once and for all, to be good
  And not bad. I'd rather be lashed by the tongue than the wood.
  As for meal, I find it more pleasant to eat than to grind it.

Therefore, I always comply with the will of my lord
Calmly, and well I preserve it; and I can afford
To deserve whatever I get by way of reward.
Let others look after their interests; they'll find a good way.
But this is how to serve your man best. That's what I say.
Let me always be careful, and pretty darn prayerful
Not to get in any trouble, so that I'll always be there, full
Of energy, coming in on the double where he needs me most,
His assistant host. Slaves who keep themselves good and scared
When they're not in the wrong usually find that they are declared
Highly usable by their owners. The fearless ones are the goners;
When it comes time to face the music, these singsongers
Will be cheeping like jailbirds and wishing they weren't such
 gone-wrongers.
But I don't have to worry much longer, not me.
The time's almost here now when he promised to set me free.
That's how I slave and work well, and how I decide
To do the best thing and take the best care of my hide.
   Sooooo . . . now that I've seen all the baggage and the
   porters in their bedding
In the tavern downtown, as Menaechmus instructed, I'm heading
Back to meet him. Guess I'll knock on the door
So he'll know I'm out here and get up off the floor
Or at least let me pull him outside
From this den of iniquity, now that he's tried
To have a good time, and probably found out the cost.
I hope I'm not too late and that the battle's not already lost.

Scene Six

[OLD MAN, WHIPSTERS, MESSENIO, *and* MENAECHMUS I]

OLD MAN Now I tell you, by all that's human or holy, make sure
 You carry out my orders just right as I ordered you to
 And order you now. You're to heft that man on your shoulders
 And hustle him off to the clinic, if you don't want your legs
 And your back pounded in. And don't pay the least attention,
 Any one of you, to anything he says. Well, don't just stand there.
 What are you waiting for? You ought to be after him, lifting him.
 I'll trot on over to the doctor's and be there when you pull in.

MENAECHMUS I Well I'll be *God* damned! What's on the schedule
 now?
 Why are these men rushing at me, what in the name of . . . ?
 What do you guys want? What's all the racket about?
 Why are you closing in on me all of a sudden? What's the hurry?

Where we going? Some rumble. Creepers! They're giving me the
tumble.
God *damn* us! Citizens all, of Epidamnus! To the rescue!
Save me, my fellow men! Help! Let go me, you whipster
bastards.

MESSENIO   Holy smoke! Creepers! What's this bunch of gypsters
think
They're gonna get away with? My master? Why those hijacking
lifters,
They've got him on their shoulders. Let's see who gets the most
blisters.

MENAECHMUS I   Won't *anyone* lend me a hand?

MESSENIO   I will sir, at your command;
You brave Captain. Boy, this is gonna give Epidamnus a black
eye,
A mugging like this, right out in the open. *Epidam-nee-ee-ee-I!*
My master's being towed away in broad daylight, a free man
Who came to your city in peace, attacked on the street. *Can*
Anybody help us? Stay off, you lugs. Lay off.

MENAECHMUS I   Hey, for God's sake, whoever you are, help me
out,
Won't you? Don't let them get away with murder. You can see
I'm in the right.

MESSENIO   Quite. Of course I'll pitch in
And come to your defense and stand by you with all my might.
I'd never let you go under, Commander, I'd sink first.
Now you sink your fist in that guy's eye . . . No, not that one,
The one who's got you by the shoulder. That's it. Now a bolder
Swipe at the ball, gouge it out for him. I'll start distributing
A crack in the puss here, a sock in the jaw there. I'm at liberty
To do so? By the heavyweight Hercules, you thugs are gonna
lug
Him away like a carload of lead, today. You'll pay by the ounce
When you feel my fists bounce all over your faces. Let go his
grace.

MENAECHMUS I   I've got this guy's eye.

MESSENIO   Make like it's just a hole in his head.
You're a bunch of bums, you body snatching, loot-latching whipsters.

WHIPSTER I   Hey, this wasn't what the doctor ordered, was it, or
the old mister?

WHIPSTER II   They didn't say we'd be on the receiving end, did
they . . . ouch!

Gee Hercules, Jerkules, that hurt!

MESSENIO Well, let him loose, then.

MENAECHMUS I How dare this ape lay hands on me? Bongo him,
jungle boy.

MESSENIO Here we go, kids, you too; take off, fade out, monkey
face;
Get the crucified cross of a holy hell and gone out of here.
You too, take that, you vandal. Get a lift from my sandal.
You're the last one, might as well get what's left behind.
Well . . . Phew . . . ! Say, I made it, didn't I? Just about in time.

MENAECHMUS I Young man, whoever you are, may the gods al-
ways shine
On your face. If it hadn't been for you I wouldn't have lasted
Through sunset today.

MESSENIO By all that's holy, if you wanted
To reward me, oh Master, you could free me.

MENAECHMUS I Me liberate you?
I'm afraid I don't follow, young fellow. Aren't you making some
mistake?

MESSENIO Me make a mistake?

MENAECHMUS I By our father Jupiter, I swear
I am not your master.

MESSENIO Don't talk that way.

MENAECHMUS I I'm not lying.
No slave of mine ever helped me as you did today.

MESSENIO Well, then, let me go free, even if you say you don't
know me.
Then I won't be yours.

MENAECHMUS I But of course! Far as I'm concerned,
Thou art henceforth free—and thou mayest go wherever thou
wantest to.

MESSENIO You say that officially?

MENAECHMUS I Hercules, yes. In my official capacity,
Insofar as that governs you.

MESSENIO Thanks very much.
And greetings, dear patron! Now that I'm free to be your client
And depend on you on equal terms. [*turns to audience*]

> *Gaudete! He's free today!*
> *Good show for Messenio!*
> *Aren't you all glad he's let go?*

[Audience cheers and applauds—and that is some *stage direction.]*

> *[still to audience]* Well, I guess I'll accept it from you; thanks
> for the congratulations.
> You've all given me quite a hand. I feel *man you mitted.*
> But, Menaechmus, my patron, I'm just as much at your service
> As I was when I used to be your slave. I want to stay by you.
> And when you go home I want to go with you too.

MENAECHMUS I *[aside]*   God, no! Not another client.

MESSENIO   I'll ankle downtown
> To the tavern and bring back the baggage and cash. That purse
> I hid away and locked in the trunk with the traveler's checks.
> I'll go get it now and deliver it all back to you.

MENAECHMUS I   Oh yes, do bring that.

MESSENIO   I'll bring it all back intact
> Just as you handed it over. You wait here for me. *[Exit]*

MENAECHMUS I   There's a bumper crop of miracles manifesting
> marvels by the millions
> Around here today: some people saying I'm not who I am
> And keeping me out from where I belong; then comes along
> This slave who says he belongs to me, whom I've just set free.
> Now he says he'll go bring me back a purseful of cash;
> And if he does that I'll insist he feel perfectly free
> To take leave of me and go where he wants, just in case
> When he comes to his senses he begins asking back for the
> dough.
> The doctor and my father-in-law, though, claim I'm out of my
> head.
> At least, that's what they said. It's all very hard to get hold of,
> Like a dream you dream you're having or are just being told of.
>   Oh well, I'll go on in here to visit my mistress, even though
> She's provoked at me, and do my best to prevail
> On her to give back the dress. I can certainly use it as bail
> To get off the street and into my house, *id est,* my jail.

Scene Seven

[MENAECHMUS II and MESSENIO]

MENAECHMUS II   You have the nerve to be telling me you reported
> back to me
> Since the time I sent you away and told you to meet me?

MESSENIO   Exactly. Only a moment ago I saved you from destruc-
tion
At the hands of those four whipsters hoisting you on their
shoulders
And carting you off, right in front of this house. You were letting
out
Loud shouts, calling on all the gods and on men,
When I roared in and pulled you loose by sheer brute strength
And knocked the block off them all, much to their surprise.
And for the service I rendered in saving you, you set me free.
Then I told you I'd go get the baggage and our cash—and then
you
Doubled round the corner as fast as you could, to meet me
And deny the whole thing.

MENAECHMUS II   I told you you could be free?

MESSENIO.   Positive.

MENAECHMUS II   I'm more positive still that before I'd see
You turned free man I'd turn into a slave, yes me, man.

Scene Eight

[MESSENIO, MENAECHMUS I, *and* MENAECHMUS II]

MENAECHMUS I [*comes out of* DÉSIRÉE'S *house*]   You can swear
by your two jaundiced eyes if you want, that won't
Make it any more true that I took away the dress and bracelet
today,
You whole bunch of blue-eyed, organized man-eaters for pay.

MESSENIO   Heavens to . . . let's see . . . What's this I see?

MENAECHMUS II   So, what
Do you see?

MESSENIO   Your looking glass, boss.

MENAECHMUS II   You mean to say what?

MESSENIO   I say I see your reflection over there. I could swear
It's your face exactly.

MENAECHMUS II   God, if it isn't like me,
When I stop to consider how I look.

MENAECHMUS I   Oh boy, there, whoever you are,
You saved my life. Glad to see you.

MESSENIO   Young man, I wonder
If you'd mind telling me what your name is, by God in heaven?

MENAECHMUS I   Heavenly God, no, of course I don't mind. The favor
You did me rates in return my nonreluctant behavior:
After all, you're my savior. I go by the name of Menaechmus.

MENAECHMUS II   So do I, for God's sake.

MENAECHMUS I   I'm Sicilian, from Syracuse.

MENAECHMUS II   And my native city is the same.

MENAECHMUS I   What's that you claim?

MENAECHMUS II   Only what's the truth.

MESSENIO   I can tell you which is which easily.
I'm his slave [points to MENAECHMUS I], but I thought all along
I was his.
And I thought you were him. That's why I talked back that way.
Please excuse me if I've spoken too stupidly for words to you.

MENAECHMUS II   You're raving right now. Think back. Remember how
You got off the ship with me today?

MESSENIO   A fair enough question.
I'll change my mind. You're my master and I am your slave.
So long, you. Good afternoon, again, to you. And I mean you.
I say, this one's Menaechmus.

MENAECHMUS I   I say that's me.

MENAECHMUS II   What's the story, you? Menaechmus?

MENAECHMUS I   Yep. Menaechmus. Son of Moschus.

MENAECHMUS II   You're my father's son?

MENAECHMUS I   No, fellow, *my* father's. I'm not
After yours. I don't want to hop on yours and take him from you.

MESSENIO   By all the gods, all over heaven, can my mind
Be sure of what it hopes for so desperately? *I've got 'em untwined:*
These men are the two twins who separately now are combined
To recall the same father and fatherland they shared in their likeness.
I'll speak to my master. Ahoy there, Menaechmus.

MENAECHMUS I *and* MENAECHMUS II [*together*]   What is it?

MESSENIO   No, no, not both. I only want my shipmate.

MENAECHMUS I   Not me.

MENAECHMUS II   But me.

MESSENIO   You're the one I must talk to. Come here.

MENAECHMUS II   Here I am. What's up?

MESSENIO   That man's either your absolute brother
Or an absolute fake. I never saw one man look more like an-
other.
Water's no more like water, or milk more like milk
Than you two drops of the same identical ilk.
Besides, he cites the same fatherland and father.
Don't you think investigating further might be worth the
bother?

MENAECHMUS II   Say, that's very good advice you're giving me.
Thanks very much.
Keep boring in, I implore you, by Hercules' knee.
If you come up with my brother, I fully intend to see
That *thou shalt go free.*

MESSENIO   I hope I come out right in the end.

MENAECHMUS II   I hope the same thing for you.

MESSENIO [*to* MENAECHMUS I]   Now, fellow, what do you say?
Menaechmus, I believe that is what you said you were called.

MENAECHMUS I   Right you are.

MESSENIO   Now this fellow here has the name of Menaechmus,
Just like you, and you said you were born at Syracuse.
So was he. Now both of you pay close attention to me,
And see if what I work out doesn't prove well worth it.

MENAECHMUS I   You've already earned the right to whatever you
want
From me. You've only to ask and you'll gain it. If it's money
You want, I'm ready to supply it. Just ask. I won't deny it.

MESSENIO   I am hopeful at the moment of setting about to dis-
cover
The fact that you two are twins, born for each other
And on the same day to the very same father and mother.

MENAECHMUS I   That sounds miraculous. I wish you could keep
that promise.

MESSENIO   I'll come through all right. Now listen here, each one
of you
To just what I say. And answer my questions in turn.

MENAECHMUS I   Ask what you will. I'll answer and never keep
back
Anything I know.

MESSENIO   Is your name Menaechmus?

MENAECHMUS I   I admit it.

MESSENIO   Is that your name too?

MENAECHMUS II   So it is.

MESSENIO   You say that your father
Was Moschus?

MENAECHMUS I   So I do.

MENAECHMUS II   Me too.

MESSENIO   You're from Syracuse?

MENAECHMUS I   That I am.

MESSENIO   How about you?

MENAECHMUS II   Naturally, me too.

MESSENIO   So far, it all checks perfectly. Now let's forge ahead.
Tell me, how far back do you remember having been in your
country?

MENAECHMUS I   Well, I remember the day I went to Tarentum,
to the fair
And wandered off away from my father among some men who
took me
And brought me here.

MENAECHMUS II Jupiter One and Supreme, that can only mean . . . !

MESSENIO   What's all the racket? Can't you pipe down? Now, how
old
Were you when your father took you with him from Sicily?

MENAECHMUS I   Seven. I was just beginning to lose my first teeth,
And I never saw my father again.

MESSENIO   Here's another question:
How many sons did your father have?

MENAECHMUS I   Two, to my knowledge.

MESSENIO   Were you the older, or was the other?

MENAECHMUS I   Both the same age.

MESSENIO   That's impossible.

MENAECHMUS I   I mean, we were twins.

MENAECHMUS II   The gods are on my side.

MESSENIO   If you keep interrupting, I'll stop.

MENAECHMUS II   No, no. I'll be quiet.

MESSENIO   Tell me, did you both have the same name?

MENAECHMUS I   Not at all. I had
The name I have now, Menaechmus. They called him Sosicles.

MENAECHMUS II   The lid's off! I just can't keep from hugging him
hard.
My own twin brother, *ciao!* It's me: Sosicles!

MENAECHMUS I   How come you changed your name to Menaechmus?

MENAECHMUS II   After they told us how you had been taken away
From our father, and carried off by strangers, and father died,
Our grandfather gave me your name. He made the changes.

MENAECHMUS I   I bet that's just how it happened. But tell me
something.

MENAECHMUS II   Ask me something.

MENAECHMUS I   What was our dear mother's name?

MENAECHMUS II   Henrietta Battleship.

MENAECHMUS I   That's it, all right. Never on a diet.
Oh, *brother,* this is a riot. I just *cain't* keep quiet.
Imagine meeting you here after all these years, I mean
I never thought I'd ever lay eyes on you again, much less
Wring your neck, you old numero *uno,* I mean *duo.*

MENAECHMUS II   Oh, you big beautiful brute you. *Et ego et tu.*
You know
How long I've been hunting for you, and how much trouble
I've gone to to locate my double! I'm glad to be here, lad.

MESSENIO   You see, boss, that's why that mercenary much of a
wench in there
Called you by his name. She thought he was you when she
hauled
You in to dinner.

MENAECHMUS I   As a matter of heavenly fact, I did order dinner
set up
Behind my wife's back, right here today, and sneaked out a dress,
And gave it to Désirée.

MENAECHMUS II   Wouldn't be this dress, brother,
Would it?

MENAECHMUS I   That's it, brother. But how did you happen to
come by it?

MENAECHMUS II   I just happened to come by and the girlfriend
pulled me in to dinner
And said I'd given her the dress. I dined very well,
I wined like a lord, I reclined with my refined escort.

Then I took away the dress, and this gold bracelet too.

MENAECHMUS I   Good for you,
Old boy. Because of me, you've at least enjoyed
Your day in Epidamnus. I'm glad of that. Now, when she
Called you in, she of course, thought sure you were me.

MESSENIO   Ahem! Need I wait much longer to be free as you commanded?

MENAECHMUS I   Brother, he's asking for only what is his just due.
Just do it
For my sake, won't you?

MENAECHMUS II   *Thou art henceforth free.*

MENAECHMUS I
        Gaudete! He's free today!
        Good show for Messenio!
        Aren't you all glad he's let go?

MESSENIO   Congratulations are all very fine, but perhaps something more *exchangeable*
Like, say, money, will make a free future not only assured but *manageable*.

MENAECHMUS II   Now, brother, everything's finally worked out so well,
Let's both go back to our homeland.

MENAECHMUS I   I'll do anything you wish,
Brother. I'll have a big auction here and sell all I own.
Meanwhile, temporarily, here we go home rejoicing.

MENAECHMUS II   I'm with you.

MESSENIO   I've a favor to ask.

MENAECHMUS I   Don't hesitate.

MESSENIO   Appoint me auctioneer.

MENAECHMUS I   Sold! To the former slave!

MESSENIO   Well, shall I announce the sale then?

MENAECHMUS I   Sure, for a week from today.

MESSENIO [*to audience*]   Big auction at Menaechmus' house a
week from today!
Must sell slaves, furniture, town house, country estate!
Everything's going, everything, for whatever you can pay!
He'll even sell the wife to any buyer willing to try her.
We'll make a million dollars and we may even go higher
If you count my commission. All invited! It ought to be great!
—But, oh, wait, Spectators! Don't forget the theater's laws.
We'll leave you first, on a burst of good loud applause!

CHANDLER EDITIONS IN DRAMA
Robert W. Corrigan, *Editor*

Other Continental and Classical are listed inside the front cover.